Introduction
to African culture:
general aspects

Alpha I. Sow, Ola Balogun,
Honorat Aguessy and Pathé Diagne

960
I61-T

Published in 1979 by the United Nations
Educational, Scientific and Cultural Organization
7 Place de Fontenoy, 75700 Paris
Printed by Presses Universitaires de France, Vendôme

ISBN: 92-3-101478-1   82-4619

Preface

Increasingly today culture is being recognized as an indispensable aspect of authentic development. This recent tendency is reflected, in many countries throughout the world, in the emergence of institutions designed to promote culture.

In the former colonies, especially in Africa, culture has played a vital role in the struggle for national liberation. Since independence, the assertion of a cultural identity has been one of the top priority goals of all African States.

Thus far, however, there has been no widely available general work on African culture for African and non-African readers. This *Introduction to African Culture* is intended to fill that gap.

The following essays were commissioned by Unesco and were specially written for this volume by African scholars who, from their different viewpoints, have striven to outline a rational approach to African culture. Studies of specific cultural themes and the various geographic areas of African culture will follow in separate publications.

In the 'Prolegomena', Alpha Sow opens the discussion with a presentation of theoretical and methodological questions raised by African culture in contemporary Africa; and he then outlines a proposal for a new cultural programme.

In 'Form and Expression in African Arts', Ola Balogun introduces the reader to the African conception of art, and to its dynamics and modes of expression.

Following, Honorat Aguessy, in his 'Traditional African Views and Apperceptions', starts out by examining some of the conclusions about African culture drawn by representative figures of European scholarship, and then urges us to approach the African cultures from a new perspective.

Finally, Pathé Diagne analyses both the cultural and political trends which have affected the evolution of African culture from the first struggles against colonialism to the assertion of cultural identity, via the key concepts of Negritude and the African personality.

It goes without saying that these four African academics have given us their personal views on African culture and its part in the African and world destinies, and consequently they are solely responsible for the ideas advanced here.

Contents

Contents

Prolegomena

Alpha I. Sow

*Our own monuments are oral traditions
which die along with the old men, conveyed
by a multitude of languages which often
do not communicate.*

*Our traditional authorities no longer
have any responsibility or any means of
expression. Our institutions are undergoing
the aggressive irruption of modernity. We
are in the world a fragile people.*[1]

Within the framework of the programme of 'Studies on African Cultures', approved by the eighteenth session of the Unesco General Conference, the decision was taken to publish 'an *Introduction to African Culture* intended for the general public' which would deal with 'the literatures, arts and cultural values of traditional and modern Africa'.[2]

The present book is intended to answer the need thus acknowledged for a presentation of the authentic values of the African cultural heritage in both their diversity and their points in common. Its purpose is to acquaint the general public throughout the world with those values and hence to further international understanding and co-operation.

The general reader tends to embarrass specialists by asking for clear-cut simple answers to generally complex and controversial questions, which are often still matters of scholarly investigation (or matters about which hasty and highly personal judgements are made). The Negro-African cultural heritage arouses a good deal of lively interest; indeed many people want to understand its fundamental significance, its history and its most characteristic forms of expression. And as the Black African States emerge and develop this interest increases.

1. From an interview with Alioune Diop in *ICAM-Information*, No. 2, March, 1976, p. 30.
2. cf. Document 18C/5, Unesco, 1975, p. 302.

Alpha I. Sow

But it may be asked whether national sovereignty has in fact liberated and enhanced cultures which the colonial powers had formerly stiffled or disfigured. One would like to know if the people's culture, which was only yesterday ignored or rejected, is able to blossom out today. Why are the African languages and cultures, which are studied and appreciated mostly outside Africa, considered and presented merely as ethnographic documents? How is it that, even in this post-colonial age, the participation of African intellectuals in the ideological discussions of the culture of their own people remains minimal? Why is it that the great collectors, critics and theoreticians of Negro-African art are invariably Westerners? How has it come to pass that civilizations which gave rise to great works of art in prehistoric times and throughout antiquity and the precolonial era—cultures which produced the African rock-drawings and paintings and engravings, the art of the Great Kingdoms, and all the bronze objects and figurines now displayed in the European and American museums—how is it that they declined to the point where they allowed themselves to be conquered and outdistanced.

In the intellectual, artistic and literary fields, can one speak of a body of specific values on which a common cultural identity for Black Africa might be based, as is the case for the Western and Arab countries?

CULTURAL ISSUES
IN CONTEMPORARY AFRICA

Though recognizing the fact that 'in Africa, cultural diversity reflected a living reality',[1] the delegates to the Intergovernmental Conference on Cultural Policies in Africa

affirmed that unity was the primary goal. In this connection, they stressed the necessity of identifying the African cultures' common points, which constitute a basis for Africanism.[2]

Likewise, the young Africans who met in Abomey under the auspices of Unesco concluded that, despite incontrovertible cultural diversity

---

1. *Intergovernment Conference on Cultural Policies in Africa. Final report*, sect. 35, p. 7, Paris, Unesco, 1975.
2. ibid., p. 7–8, sect. 37.

'that was apparent in regard to languages, the arts, musical traditions, religious beliefs, etc.'[1] similarities between the different peoples of the continent nevertheless existed.

They had grown up through the course of history as a result of manifold human, religious or commercial contacts which had contributed to the forging of deep ties among African peoples both prior to and after colonization.[2]

The participants of the regional meeting of Abomey also pointed out that some foreign observers

had developed the habit of representing the multiplicity of their cultures to Africans as a bogy and a fundamental obstacle to their rapprochement.

Such observers were primarily anxious, if not to denigrate African cultures, at least to thrust them into the background—when they did not relegate them to the status of sub-cultures.[3]

The positions and beliefs which I have just summarized bring us to the heart of a debate, which is still confused, and studded with contradictions and arguments, not only among the African ideologists, but also among the various representatives of the Westernized African élites. Indeed, as we shall see later, most thinking about the traditional African cultures is being done by non-Africans. In the case of cultures which the official school refuses to recognize, cultures whose keepers do not hold positions in the economic or political structures of the new States (the power of decision over essential questions no longer being placed in their hands), a large number of Westernized African intellectuals simply overlook them[4] or do not believe in their importance. Instead they see only outdated religious practices, initiation symbols, ill-assorted and purely functional cult objects, folktales and proverbs, superstition and magic.

1. *Young People and African Cultural Values*, p. 114, Paris, Unesco, 1975.
2. ibid., p. 115.
3. ibid., p. 114.
4. In *L'Afrique Révoltée*, p. 144–5 (Paris, Présence Africaine, 1958), Albert Tévoedjré writes, '. . . though I study French, that so perfect language, with a great deal of interest, I will always regret the fact that I was obliged to learn French first, to think in French, to remain ignorant of my mother tongue; I will always deplore the fact that I was forced to become a stranger in my own country!'

Alpha I. Sow

As a result, it is mainly Western intellectuals like Baumann and Westermann,[1] Forde,[2] Murdock,[3] Herskovits,[4] Maquet,[5] and others, who have tried, each in turn, to identify those cultural features and civilizational traits which are common to the various African societies. Despite the fact that their methods are currently being disputed by other scholars, and despite the fact that the identity of African man as they characterize it appears to be of dubious authenticity, they have at least performed the invaluable service of suggesting the bare outlines of a synthesis which includes the different African cultures and defines their common features.[6]

Negritude and the Negro-African cultural identity

The individuation of cultures, the respect for their specific differences, is one of the fundamental demands of our century. In many Third World countries, it has led to an assertion of national identity, which is conceived of as a form of collective self-defence, a condition for survival to counteract the inevitable disintegration resulting from dehumanizing mechanization and uncontrolled and generalized industrialization.

It seems that in Black Africa this concept means a futile reversion to Negritude instead of truly positive development—that is to say fruitful change and growth.

Whether it is praised and defended, or redeemed, disputed, or else rejected, Negritude invariably arouses strong feelings, and in every case produces strange misunderstandings. Historical Negritude had defined, extolled and enhanced the specific identity traits of black peoples at grips with the socio-cultural violence of slavery and

1. H. Baumann and D. Westermann, *Les Peuples et les Civilisations de l'Afrique*, Paris, Payot, 1948.
2. International African Institute, *African Worlds*, London, Oxford University Press, 1954.
3. G. P. Murdock, *Africa: Its Peoples and their Culture History*, New York, McGraw, 1959.
4. M. J. Herskovits, *The Human Factor in Changing Africa*, New York, Knopf, 1962.
5. J. Maquet, *Les Civilisations Noires*, Verviers, Gérard, 1966.
6. In an article for the *Encyclopedia Universalis* (Vol. 1, Paris, 1968, p. 405–7), Jacques Maquet distinguishes five main civilizations in Black Africa: the civilization of the bow and arrow, the civilization of the forest clearings, the civilization of the graneries, the civilization of the lance and the civilization of the cities.

colonialism; it had presented itself as a profoundly *disalienating* doctrine of struggle. In its wake, we are witnessing the emergence of a kind of neo-Negritude which sees itself as contributing feeling, soul and intuition to the West. Squarely serving the interests of neo-colonialism, which uses it, this latter-day Negritude redeems the Afro-colonial urban culture which has been undeservedly promoted to the rank of a national culture; it easily turns into an obscurantist native technique for exerting power, and it hampers the liberation and the social advancement of the black peoples.

In an article published in 1970 in *AfricAsia*,[1] the Haitian militant, René Depestre outlines the historical features of the concept of Negritude. Though he condemns and attacks the politically and culturally oppressive and reactionary intention behind the notion of 'epidermizing Negritude', or the 'imprisoning' or 'debilitating' concept of a certain kind of Negritude, he does not altogether reject the ideology. He extols and defends its progressive, nationalistic and disalienating tendencies and historical orientation. In contrast to a 'warped Negritude', which he rejects, he distinguishes and argues for an authentic and positive Negritude.

In Roumain and his best disciples, Negritude was a concept of national liberation, an enlightening, unifying concept, a sort of new ideological 'maroonism', which, while subscribing to Marxism, added the charm of our Caribbean peculiarities to the latter's wealth.

In Franz Fanon, Negritude took the twofold character of alienation among the oppressed black peoples into consideration, and presented itself as the emotional reaction of the exploited and humiliated black man.

With Aimé Césaire, the father of this concept, which he defended and made famous throughout a long and exemplary series of writings, Negritude was above all a concrete realization of being oppressed (as it was too with Guillén, Fanon, Roumain, Damas and others), that is to say a deeply emotional quest for identity in the black man degraded by centuries of scorn and slavery.[2]

To be sure, as a mobilizing cultural and political manifesto, Negritude shaped the socio-cultural identity of the black peoples

1. R. Depestre, 'Haïti ou la Négritude Dévoyée', *AfricAsia*, Nos. 5 and 6, January, 1970.
2. ibid., No. 6, p. 35.

into a weapon for achieving emancipation and a programme of cultural rebirth. It fought Eurocentrism, racism and the prejudices, lack of understanding and arrogance of the triumphant colonial powers. It rejected acculturation, assimilation and alienation. It demystified the Western cultural paradigm taken as a universal frame of reference. It vigorously asserted the right to be different, and it acquainted Negroes with the still novel concept of cultural relativity. By giving the colonized black peoples a clear sense of themselves, of their racial solidarity and of their situation, it restored their national pride and helped to link them to their history, their cultural traditions and their languages. And the return to Negro-African origins sanctioned 'the Negro civilizational values'. As a result, Negritude made it possible to weld the consciousness of the black peoples together and to mobilize them for the struggle against colonialism and for liberation.

Nevertheless, a number of African intellectuals are of the opinion today that Negritude no longer has a historical role to play as an ideology for struggle and as a useful, that is to say a mobilizing, programme of cultural and political rebirth. In overthrowing the old type of colonialism, the national liberation struggles gave certain pioneers, theoreticians and movement leaders an opportunity to exercise substantial political power, to which they gave an orientation favourable to neo-colonialism. Thereby disqualified as leaders of the nationalist movements, they soon became the targets of these movements. At their instigation, a 'warped Negritude' emerged, which reduced the struggle of the black peoples, at the moment it was actually intensifying, to a literary debate—one that was all the more devoid of content in that it was confined to a handful of Westernized Negro intellectuals. These political allies of a system which exploits and oppresses their people, have become the protagonists of a diversionary form of Negritude which can only lead to a dead-end.

There are some ideologists, doubtless newcomers to a struggle whose basic character and historical successes they are ignorant of, who seem intent on fighting battles which have already been won. Thus they want contemporary Africa to revert to its pre-colonial roots in order to extract itself from the influence of Western culture. They even suggest substituting 'cultural identity' for Negritude!

True, the cultural identity of the black peoples had been denied and derided by the colonial powers. But it is absurd to attempt to mobilize the African nations fifteen years after they have acquired independence for this verification of cultural identity, given the fact that the Negritude movement has already successfully combated the universalist cultural claims of Eurocentrism, and has already enhanced the Negro civilizations.

Today it seems far more important to study the ideological foundations, the contents and the historical development of the Negritude movement, and to assess it within the context of the cultural rebirth of the black peoples, than to try and assert a cultural identity that is too general and superficial to be of any real consequence to Africans and to mobilize them.

Negritude, 'Africanity' and 'Arabness'

Since the founding of the Organization of African Unity (OAU) in 1963, the need to establish a cultural basis for that continent-wide intergovernmental institution has led a number of Africans to devise a new ideology, 'Africanity'. This is presented as 'the body of common points among the African cultures'. Thus Africanity looks beyond 'petty local differences' and stresses a 'fundamental identity'. It rests on the authority of the *Cultural Manifesto* of the first Pan-African Festival of Algiers, and from the start it defined itself as an alternative to Negritude, one of the great moments of which was undoubtedly the first World Black and African Festival of Arts and Culture held in Dakar in 1965.

Defining the purpose and the scope of the world festival, Alioune Diop declared:

The idea is essentially to give an opportunity to black communities throughout the world to consult together in order to revitalize their culture, their creativity so as to balance and expand the International Society, because it is up to our peoples to share with the other peoples around the world, the responsibility of managing the world which is our common weal.[1]

---

1. A. Diop, *AfricAsia*, No. 6, p. 29.

Alpha I. Sow

Whereas historical Pan-Africanism was a political and cultural movement comparable to what Pan-Arabism was in the Arab countries, the new Pan-Africanism which emerged at the Algiers festival now presents itself as the political foundation of an inter-African institution which is as yet only a goal. Some leaders in post-colonial Africa want to establish Africanity as the cultural basis for this political ideal. They therefore equate the African socio-cultural entities with the geo-political divisions made by the colonial powers. They refuse the concepts of 'Negro-African culture' and 'Arab-Berber culture', which they view as abstractions detrimental to African unity, and accuse them of being encouraged by neo-colonial interests. They believe that

Africa as a whole constitutes a single cultural family, and that there was no need to create a dichotomy which would be an obstacle to African unity.[1]

True, there is no denying the fact that the African peoples share a rich common cultural heritage, that they are linked by a sense of solidarity shaped by the experience of anti-colonial struggle, and that they have a common determination to unite against the ever-present threat of imperialism (despite their recently acquired political independence, which has to be consolidated). But rather than hastening to merge, would it not be wiser to begin by delimiting the African cultures clearly, and thereby establishing a better basis for unity? As Léopold Senghor says:

If we want to build a *united* Africa, we must make certain it will be a firmly united Africa, and therefore we must base it on our common cultural traits and not on our political differences. I have said that there are two cleavages, two stumbling blocks to African unity. There is the division between English-speaking and French-speaking countries, and there is the division between Arab-Berbers and Negro-Africans. The latter seems to me the more formidable, because it is the oldest and because it derives from the ambivalent nature of Africa itself.[2]

1. *Intergovernmental Conference on Cultural Policies in Africa. Final Report*, op. cit., p. 8, sect. 38.
2. Speech delivered at the University of Cairo on 16 February 1967, in the presence of Gamal Abdel Nasser and several Egyptian ministers, on the occasion of the

Prolegomena

Summing up and concluding his speech, Senghor stresses the following point:

On the one hand, we have to remain ourselves, and on the other hand we must open ourselves to the other. This we must do in order *to give and to receive*. You must remain *Arabs*, otherwise you will have nothing to offer us. And when I say Arabs, I am not even referring to *Arabism*, which is a programme, a will to action; I am speaking of *Arabness*, that Arabness which is the hearth whence the virtues of the eternal Bedouin radiate. As for us, who live south of the Sahara, we must remain Negroes. And I mean precisely Negro-Africans. That is to say, each day we must slake our thirst at the gushing springs of rhythm and the image-symbol, of love and of faith. But, in giving, we must also be capable of receiving.[1]

The Arab States of Africa have acknowledged the necessity, in the present stage of history, of respecting this cultural dichotomy, which a few muddled ideologists want to deny Black Africa. That is why, in 1970, these States founded the Arab Educational, Cultural and Scientific Organization (ALECSO). Among other activities, this organization promotes 'research into the cultural values of the Arab civilization and their impact on Arab youth'. It also participates in 'preserving the cultural heritage of the Arab Nation', in particular by compiling 'various guides to the libraries, museums and Arab study information centres'.

Arab intellectuals are currently raising questions of cultural rebirth similar to those discussed by their Negro-African brothers. Thus, in his opening speech for the Collective Consultation on Contemporary Arab Culture organized by ALECSO and Unesco in Cairo in June 1974, Abdel Aziz El-Sayed, the Director General of ALECSO, declared:

Culture . . . has a specific identity connected with the most intimate essence of a people, with the nature of its thought and heritage, with its

awarding of a Ph.D. *honoris causa* by the rector of the university. The text of this speech has been published under the title, *Les Fondements de l'Africanité ou Négritude et Arabité*, Paris, Présence Africaine, 1967. The passage quoted is on p. 103.

1. ibid., p. 103–4.

perception of things and its way of looking at them. It is culture that distinguishes peoples from one another; however, this distinction—in the case of 'open' human cultures such as that of the Arabs—does not preclude contacts and encounters with other peoples: on the contrary, it invites such contacts and encounters, and indeed imposes and prescribes them. It is this that gives rise to the great cultural questions such as authenticity and renewal or unity and diversity. These questions are nowadays the subject of continuing debate and study among men of culture, thinkers, writers and artists in the countries of the Arab nation. It would not have been possible for such questions to arise in an enclosed culture, self-absorbed and restricted in its range; nor would it have been possible for them to arise in a brand-new, contemporary culture without an ancient heritage and deep roots. If we do not shrink from confronting such questions and the debates and discussions surrounding them, it is because we know that our Arab culture is human and open, and that over the centuries it has constantly renewed itself within the framework of its own essential nature, and has therefore constantly been both a recipient and a benefactor; and because we know, too, that it has consistently rejected rigid moulds and uniform approaches, preferring variety within the general framework of its unity, and has therefore never failed in vigour and development.[1]

Moreover, in order to increase Arab participation in international cultural co-operation, the participants of the above meeting decided to ask Unesco to associate ALECSO and the Arab States in its programmes relating to the Culture of Central Asia, of Africa and of Europe ('with special reference to the Mediterranean and its islands').[2] Among the Unesco programmes which 'afford opportunities of creating links between Arab and other cultures', they singled out

programmes relating to Africa, e.g. the programme for a General History of Africa, the ten-year plan for the promotion of African languages, and the participation of certain African Arab States in cultural development and cultural policy programmes in Africa.[3]

---

1. *Collective Consultation on Contemporary Arab Culture, Cairo, June, 1974, Final Report and Recommendations*, p. 9, Paris, Unesco, November, 1974 (SHC–74/W S/25).
2. ibid., p. 17.
3. ibid., p. 19.

Prolegomena

Speaking of the Arab-Berber influence on Negro-Africa, Léopold Senghor has written:

I need hardly dwell on the fact that this influence is manifest in our religious life, for more than one-third of Black Africa is Moslem; in the languages, of the Cushites and Upper-Sudanese, whose religious vocabulary, even among Christians, is often of Semitic or Berber stock; in our customs, and, most important of all, in our ways of thinking.[1]

In final analysis, therefore, no theoretical incompatibility exists between the socio-cultural entities which constitute Africanity. Indeed no proponent of Negritude has ever asserted the contrary. None the less, unity does not erase diversity and should not prevent it from being acknowledged. This diversity, which pertains to the nature of things and the historical development of peoples, should never become a goal in itself. Still less should it be substituted for the symbiosis which is our aim. Political differences, which after all are often of a hypothetical nature, should not conceal the fact that diversity is, however, a necessary stage.

By championing Africanity against Negritude certain African intellectuals and political leaders believe that they are pleasing the Arabs and meanwhile settling a score with other Black African intellectuals and political figures. Some of them view Negritude as a defensive, racist doctrine extolling a cultural heritage whose status is questionable because it has been described and categorized through the distorting optics of European ethnologists, who have identified and interpreted its fundamental characteristics. They are not entirely wrong in maintaining that, owing to many of its original applications, Negritude derives from a typically Western statement of the African problems.

But this does not mean that these opponents of Negritude should be followed through all the meanderings of their inconsistent logic, which rejects Pan-Negroism while embracing Pan-Arabism. They claim that Negritude hampers African unity, but cannot the same thing be said about Arabism? If Africa is to unite and enhance

---

1. *Les Fondements de l'Africanité ou Négritude et Arabité*, op. cit., p. 103.

its cultural heritage only within the framework of the intergovernmental institution of the OAU and its special committees, why are the
African Arab states members of ALECSO and the Arab League, and
why do they laud 'the specific cultural values of the Arab nations',
or those of the 'Maghreb civilizations'? Some historical leaders of
Negritude can rightly be called 'zealous servants of neo-colonialism'
and dividers of the revolutionary anti-imperialist front. But the
pioneers of Arabism and the chiefs of State of the Arab League are
hardly more progressive.

All of which shows that, whereas the black communities are
unquestionably determined to enhance their cultural heritage, there
is no evidence of homogeneity of thought among the Westernized black intellectuals. Contaminated by the eclecticism of the
acculturized urban élites of the Third World, they reject the suppos-
edly reactionary and suicidal traditionalism of the non-Westernized
rural élites and are unable either to trace a relevant course of action
or to define a satisfactory cultural frame of reference. They are not
even capable of making a coherent and irrefutable distinction
between the problems of race and nation and those of class, and still
less of giving their state-of-mind a historical dimension by integrating their culture and their experience of contemporary revolutionary movements in the social practices of black people.

As Alphonse Quénum observes:

The culture of the intelligentsia cannot and must not be antithetic to
the culture of the people. Rather, it must be an offshoot of it, permanently
drawing nourishment from it so as not to become barren. Having emerged
from the people, our intelligentsia must learn how to return to the people
and become their critical consciousness, a force working against humbug
and deceit, living close to the masses, sharing their hopes and anxieties,
and giving them vent in political projects or expression in a doctrine
of renewal. . . .

In short, the culture of our intelligentsia must cease to be the
worship of knowledge as a means to power and possessions and must
become the will power which the people have been waiting for to catalyse
their aspirations and energies, in other words a mediating force.[1]

---

1. A. Quénum, 'Culture of the intelligentsia and culture of the people', in *Young
People and African Cultural Values*, op. cit., p. 36.

Prolegomena

A number of intellectuals and political cadres of post-colonial Black Africa consider that the strongly emotional and inopportune assertion of national originality and authenticity, at a time when no one seriously denies them, is actually part of a concerted effort to counteract the influence of Marxist-Leninism. The emergence of the Chinese and Vietnamese nations which have followed that line has aroused a good deal of admiration in Africa. The anti-Marxist strategy is presumably to maintain a certain level of theoretical confusion among the as yet uncommitted young people in search of a revolutionary ideology and a model for development, and to draw them away from the study of Marxism and sidetrack them in obscurantist mystification.

It is admittedly not always easy to remain impassive when considering the real trend, the political line and the behaviour of certain 'left-wing elocutionists' who assail Negritude from the viewpoint of Africanity, cultural personality and authenticity—as if there were a contradiction between those concepts—and who claim to be helping the Arabs, whereas in fact they are systematically intent on sowing the seeds of discord and misunderstanding in a ground where there should be only understanding, mutual respect and the fraternity of a common struggle.

Actually, there is some danger that the above controversy may degenerate into what Lu Sin called 'a storm in a teacup'. First, because in the course of the adventure that was colonialism, the peoples of Black Africa, always true to themselves, never ceased to express and to assert, in their protean daily struggles, their identity, their originality, their Negritude, or, if one prefers, their Negro-Africanity. Secondly, because in agreeing to fall back purely and simply on Marxist-Leninism one tends (as do a number of African intellectuals) to take shelter behind its authority and to make it an end in itself, overlooking the fact that at no point in the history of peoples has revolutionary ideology replaced as a programme of action the revolution itself. For many intellectuals and political leaders in our countries, Marxist-Leninism has nevertheless become a kind of hermetic metalanguage, a new kind of philosophy and an intellectual pastime primarily characterized by a need for displaying erudition and engaging in petty political machinations instead of being authentically concerned with revolutionary action.

Alpha I. Sow

PROPOSALS FOR A NEW PROGRAMME
OF CULTURAL ACTION

Having outlined the main cultural issues of contemporary Black Africa, it should now be pointed out that various general problems of methodology and orientation arise when it comes to enhancing and promoting the Negro-African cultural heritage. These difficulties do not occur primarily in setting up detailed programmes or in drawing up recommendations for sustained long-term plans of action.

More than ever today, it is above all the concepts of 'civilization' and 'culture'—both of which have been too unilaterally conceived during the periods of European hegemony—which have to be overhauled and redefined by our scholars in terms of the values and specific traits of our heritage. The Rwandese professor, Alexis Kagamé, has recently made a remarkable contribution in this respect, which it is to be hoped will not remain an isolated one. Attempting to give a concise definition of the notion of 'objective civilization', Professor Kagamé writes as follows:

Considered objectively, civilization is the adaptation of a human group making use of the whole range of human nature (intelligence, will, feeling and the bodily activities) to domesticate and improve the physical environment in which it dwells (climate and seasons, minerals, hydrography, animal and plant life), to protect itself from the internal causes of disintegration, to defend itself against similar groups which might otherwise absorb it, and to transmit to its offspring the sum of the experience it has received from its initiators.[1]

Before arriving at this definition, Professor Kagamé briefly discusses the components of the concept of objective civilization. He discerns eleven of them: a linguistic system; a large territory; long-standing occupation of that territory; an effective economy; both an internal and an international (or tribal and interclan) system of public law, including a system of administering justice; a system of social practice governing relations between individuals and groups; a body

1. A. Kagamé, *La Philosophie Bantu Comparée*, p. 49, Paris, Présence Africaine, 1976.

of technical knowledge corresponding to the real needs of the group; a criterion for artistic (literary, musical or plastic) works; a corpus of real and speculative scientific knowledge; a philosophical system; and, finally,

a religious system providing man with an explanation about his origins, a rule of conduct governing his relationship with the dead, with intangible and in-themselves inexplicable forces and with the eternal Being, as well as an answer to the questions of man's existence on earth and its ultimate purpose.[1]

At all events, the traditional African cultures permeate the social sphere of the individual African and are expressed in each one of his gestures. They form a part of the objective reality which he 'finds' surrounding him at birth and as he becomes 'conscious' within the physical and social world which he gradually discovers as he grows up. Even if the techniques he uses in his life within this environment develop but very slowly, even though his economic situation has changed little since the days when his ancestors were alive, his cultural values do far more than merely contribute, as has been said, to maintain and reproduce permanent social structures. On the contrary, on many occasions in the course of history, these values have caused man to disavow those structures and the relationships of production which characterize them, to alter them, and to sever the bonds which hampered their development. Thus they have given man the means to deal with new needs, and helped him gain a better understanding of the meaning of his life. They have brought him to question himself over and over within the daily circumstances of his life and in his relationship with society and with the universe. Provided that they are not viewed as a collection of automatic prescriptions and practices, these cultural values are in no way opposed to the evolution of African societies. On the contrary, they imply that evolution.

1. ibid., p. 48–9.

Alpha I. Sow

Cultural priorities

The essential matter of contemporary African culture—that is to say the themes developed in literature, the arts, music, film and the theatre of the large Black African cities—often lacks relevance and roots. It is as if the creative individuals in that urban culture wrote, painted or sculpted with one purpose in mind: that of resurrecting a certain type of Western audience's image of African peoples and of satisfying its need for escape. Availing itself of the large-scale modern means of distribution, this marginal, exotic, artificial, urban and touristic culture threatens to stifle the authentic cultural heritage of the people and to take its place. A new social order deriving from a powerful, imported civilization, with its alien frames of reference and values, would thus emerge. It would only tolerate and communicate harmless decorative motifs, traditional activities and residual traits of 'eternal Africa'—dances, expressive gestures, the gift of the gab, religiosity, sporadic enthusiasms, or, in Blyden's cruel phrase, 'rhythm, amiable mischievousness and eroticism forever in search of new sensations'.

Negro-African culture is not the folkloric *pot-pourri* assiduously cultivated by the mass media of the new States, and it will surely not be promoted within any neo-colonial framework.

I need hardly remind the reader that the primordial function of our culture has always been to convey a particular idea of man and nature, and to contribute to the harmony between them.

Negro art, the essential, authentic, classic Negro art, imitates neither reality nor the imagination. Dynamic and multidimensional, it identifies with both. Even as a court art it is always anonymous: it presents significant archetypes rather than faithful portraits. The traditional or classic Negro artist reproduces what he feels and knows rather than what he observes. A 'created creature', he is above all, to quote Amadou Hampaté Bâ's famous expression, a 'created creator'. Consequently he strives to appease, to conjure, to tame things, including death and suffering, the dark or baneful forces of the universe. He veils the inevitable so as to mitigate its impact and make it bearable with a supreme smile. He harmonizes and integrates Negro mythology, its wonder and poetry, into his artistic creations and in daily experience. As Amadou Hampaté Bâ writes:

Prolegomena

Something happened in Africa that has happened in many countries of the world. Arts became distorted and were forgotten by the people. Therefore the last masters hid them under symbols so that they should be left in peace by desecrators and, sometimes, by the temporal authorities, who were harsh towards the secret societies. In Africa these symbols came to be legends, maxims, masks, geometrical figures, and statuettes.[1]

The as yet little-known and little-studied myths, folktales, riddles, proverbs and conundrums are not always simple expressions of folk values. They are often devices for perpetuating and communicating a particular message or piece of knowledge. In Black Africa knowledge naturally assumes ridiculous or unimposing appearances in order to exclude the profane or the 'obtuse' disciples whom the teacher cannot 'open up' to the 'light' of knowledge, whose ears he cannot 'pierce'. The curious, the envious, the shallow who do not deserve to be acquainted with the secrets of nature and initiated into the mysteries: all are barred from the hidden wisdom. The acquisition of culture, in this case, actually depends on knowing how to understand allusions and hints concerning the essential matters, that is to say human relations.

Remember Kaïdara, the god of gold and knowledge, who appears in the guise of an insignificant beggar ,who desires no alms', a little old man garbed in sweat-soaked, threadbare swatches of cotton, who is so weak that he 'walks out of habit rather than out of strength'.[2] Or think of Bâgoumâwel, the master of occult knowledge, the decipherer of the divine message, in the tale called *L'Éclat de la Grande Étoile*,[3] who, in the form of a little old man, sleeps on a bed of ashes, feeds on jujubes, drinks from the hollow of his hand, spends his days in hillside caves and only returns to the village at dusk.

Faced with the rapid development of technology and with tools and machines imported from the West, the rudimentary techniques of spinning and weaving, the native crafts, the arts and popular traditions of Black Africa are losing ground to profit, efficiency and

1. A. Hampaté Bâ, 'Traditional Cultures and Social Changes', in *Young People and African Cultural Values*, op. cit., p. 38–55 (cf. also p. 42).
2. A. Hampaté Bâ, *Kaïdara*, p. 127, Paris, A. Colin, 1969.
3. A. Hampaté Bâ, *L'Éclat de la Grande Étoile Suivi du Bain Rituel*, p. 43, Paris, A. Colin, 1974.

Alpha I. Sow

adaptability; and they are being replaced by ignorance, blindness and prejudice.

The break between the traditional illiterate practitioners of these arts and crafts and the young Westernized Africans is increasingly becoming a reality. Very few young people want to learn the archaic and downgraded techniques. They are even unwilling to view them as starting-points for respectable work, or to make the effort to study them, to reflect on them critically or to renew them. There is ground for fearing that rootless and depersonalized societies will replace the older societies and swallow up their cultural heritage. As Amadou Hampaté Bâ observed:

The first great problem for modern Africans is to recognize this traditional culture themselves in order to take stock of it and so to define its nature and essential value. And the next problem is to create an intelligible language so that this culture can be brought within the reach of people who have broken with the hermetic practices of the initiation centres.[1]

Indeed a long period of investigating and studying the African cultural reality has begun for us. Most of our great civilizational values have yet to be discovered, analysed and conceptualized. This implies that, 'we, Negroes, we must proceed along the path of method—I would even say of conceptualization—which does not mean abstraction'.[2]

Great care should be taken, in the present stage of history, in defining the general trends of cultural policy and in identifying the most urgent problems facing the African societies, whose development depends on their equitable resolution. This means that the governing authorities of those countries will have to outline a clear cultural policy and will have to draw up a national cultural charter guaranteeing the respect, the dignity, the equality and the enhancement of the languages and cultures of all their ethnic communities, and specifying how these principles will be enforced.

---

1. A. Hampaté Bâ, 'Traditional Cultures and Social Changes', in *Young People and African Cultural Values*, op. cit., p. 38–55; the passage quoted is on p. 43.
2. *Les Fondements de l'Africanité ou Négritude et Arabité*, op. cit., p. 104.

Prolegomena

Cultural action

Seen in these terms, the programme of cultural action would be directed specifically towards inventorying, promoting and enhancing the cultural heritage of each community.

Inventorying the cultural heritage

It is impossible to develop harmoniously cultures and values that one knows little about, or that one attaches little importance to or that one misunderstands. In Black Africa the national cultural riches are still largely despised and ignored, except when a Western audience acknowledges some of them, which are then immediately placed on a pedestal, despite the fact that basically they are still not understood.

Priority must therefore be given to the enormous task of searching out and collecting data, this being a necessary preliminary for an unbiased and non-discriminating census of the African cultural heritage as a whole. Scholars and technicians trained in modern universities, collaborating with traditional intellectuals, rural organizers and cadres belonging to the masses could successfully undertake this part of the programme, once its guiding principles and the modalities of searching and collecting have been established by representative State institutions in concert with the fully informed, actively participating ethnic groups involved.

It will be particularly important, in establishing and carrying out these programmes of research, to give top priority to the more fragile works and cultural values, such as the oral traditions whose masters and chief repositories are dying out. These are generally chroniclers and oral historians, philosophers and thinkers well versed in the knowledge of ways and customs, musicians and expert singers of ancient and sacred songs, master craftsmen who possess the traditional technological and initiatory knowledge (gold-washers privy to 'the eleven kinds of mineral, the eleventh being gold, a metal which was magical before it became a royal attribute and, eventually, an economic factor',[1] wood-working artisans, herdsmen, fishermen, shoemakers, weavers, masons, smiths, hunters, etc.),

1. A. Hampaté Bâ, 'Traditional Cultures and Social Changes, op. cit., p. 43.

healers, dynastic bards, warriors, pastoralists, Muslem scholars and men of letters, priests of the traditional cults, etc.

In this initial phase, care should be taken to avoid making distinctions between what is considered relevant or irrelevant, useful or harmful. Indeed at this stage all that is required is to inventory, that is to say to collect and to record. This is sensitive work which calls for human sympathy, professional knowhow and considerable material support. In many instances, it may not be successful unless qualified regional organizations for promoting true inter-African co-operation are also established.

This work of searching out, collecting and recording works will naturally lead to acknowledgement of the preeminent and irreplaceable role of the African languages as sources and vehicles of the African peoples' thought and values, to protection of the rights of the holders of traditional knowledge, and to combating fraudulent or abusive exportation of the recorded cultural heritage.

Promoting cultures

Of course the programme will not cease with the collection and preservation of the cultural works and documents of the African peoples. It is not enough to keep them from vanishing and to protect them by treating them as archives, as it were. Above all they need to be rescued from neglect and anonymity. It is crucial that they be widely distributed in the form of books and periodicals, records, the theatre, photography, films, etc. They must be alloted a substantial place in the national education programmes. In short, they must be enhanced and promoted.

The governments of the post-colonial countries will have to take steps to decolonize the thinking patterns and the mentality of their citizens. They will have to define the orientation, the role and the place of cultural research both within their respective nations and on the level of Black Africa as a whole. And, finally, they will have to create institutions for carrying out this policy and administering it effectively.

Once the overall orientation has been established in close consultation with research workers, authorities and cultural cadres, a programme for publishing books and periodicals in the national languages will have to be defined and implemented. Eventually this programme will result in a systematic analysis of the collected heritage, and the preparation and publication of a series of works of general culture, such as the following:

Collections of religious and sacred texts, of folktales, fables and short stories, of proverbs, sayings, conundrums and riddles, of aphorisms and philosophical reflections, etc.

Anthologies of songs of war and love, of epic narratives, of pastoral and bucolic songs, of poems and dynastic hymns, of historical and legendary tales.

Monographs on the arts, techniques and trades.

Collections of educational games, satirical and humorous narratives.

Encyclopaedias of the ancient ways and customs.

But the cultural and political authorities will have to do more than merely encourage the production of these publications They will have to see to it that the above works are freely available; and they may even have to donate them to specific organizations and national institutions such as municipal lending libraries and cultural centres. They will have to encourage their translation into the languages of all the ethnic communities in their country, as well as into the major international languages. And they will have to provide facilities for adapting these works to radio and television distribution, to video-tapes, films, theatres, cultural records and cassettes.

By periodically organizing traditional sporting events, travelling cultural programmes, story hours for children, music, poetry and popular tradition festivals, and by giving them radio and television coverage throughout the country, as well as special video screening in cultural centres, the national authorities will ensure that works belonging to the oral traditions will have the advantages of systematic modern mass distribution.

Aside from that, the African States will have to make a concerted effort on the regional and subregional levels to establish and to maintain the organizations needed for preserving and promoting culture.

The systematic study of the oral, written (Arab and *Ajami* manuscripts of the western Sudanese Muslim scholars), archaeological, artistic and cultural riches of Black Africa, with a view to using and developing them, is a long-range task involving not only political authorities, intellectuals, traditional and modern cadres and the African masses, but also international cultural co-operation. In this respect, the ten-year plan for the study of oral traditions and the promotion of the African languages, adopted by the seventeenth session of the Unesco General Conference,[1] has already resulted in the main goals and priorities being listed and the general direction to be taken by the cultural action programmes to be outlined.

Updating cultural values

After a period of direct colonial domination during which the values of its cultural heritage were denied, derided and distorted, Black Africa certainly seeks to assert its personality, to resist the intellectual control of the Western powers and to urge a return to the original national sources rooted in its history. But it would be a dangerous mistake for it to remain uncritically satisfied with its cultural heritage. On the contrary, the various works will have to be placed back in their context, and subjected to a systematic internal and external scrutiny, so as to establish their scope and their purpose. They will have to be discussed, adapted, translated and used as bases for new creative works. In this way, not only an authentic but also a popular and progressive cultural vitality will emerge from them.

The creative activity of African artists, authors, critics, translators and adaptors will be all the more relevant, masterful and influential in so far as it will be based on well-known and thoroughly assimilated national sources and will address a demanding and well-informed audience.

By means of translations into foreign languages, and exchanges of books, periodicals and other documents, by means of radio, television and film distribution, the main representative works of African culture will be brought to those who live beyond the boundaries of the national communities whose heritage is constituted by those works. They will thus stimulate responses that will undoubtedly cause them to be improved.

To sum up, national scientific and popular cultural policies need to be defined and made operative. These policies will have to aim at

1. cf. Alpha I. Sow (ed.), *Langues et Politiques de Langues en Afrique Noire: l'Expérience de l'Unesco*, p. 432–57, Paris, Nubia, 1977.

filling the existing gaps in knowledge and in the current training systems. They will have to provide for top-priority study programmes for making the African communities known through their oral and written cultures, their fundamental works, their languages, their various literary and artistic productions. Finally they will have to indicate the priorities in organizing, enhancing and distributing the cultural common wealth.

African countries need to have access to the most advanced knowledge in order to have a truly modern agriculture, industry, science and culture. They are aspiring therefore to a cultural renaissance which, while giving Africans the chance to regain their erstwhile threatened and controverted personality and authenticity and to release their inherent dynamism, will also open up vistas which will benefit the whole world.

Form and expression in African arts

Ola Balogun

INTRODUCTION

Considerations on the nature of art

It has often been said that art is a universal language, capable of
spanning distances and of communicating an identical message to
all men irrespective of race and creed. Although this is a very
appealing image, we often find however that most works of art are
so closely related to the social, historical and cultural background
of the societies in which they have originated that they may not be
instantly comprehensible to persons not familiar with the context
out of which they have grown. In some cases, there may even be a
total loss of communication when a work of art that has originated
in a given setting is observed in an entirely different one. The language
of the work of art (in the sense of form) may thus prove totally
indecipherable where there are no commonly shared elements to
permit interpretation.

Not only is the interpretation of form a source of difficulty, but
the actual content of a work of art may remain inaccessible even
where the form has been understood. This is because even if an
understanding of the form employed in a work of art to achieve
communication can be ensured, there is no guarantee that the actual
content or message which such forms serve to vehicle will be accessible to one not familiar with the background from which the work

of art has originated. For instance, would a non-Japanese spectator watching a *No* play for the first time necessarily appreciate the depth of feeling and the philosophy that such a play seeks to convey, if he has no prior knowledge of Japanese history and culture?

We also find that aesthetic norms tend to vary considerably from one region to the other, and from age to age. To take a simple example, Renaissance aesthetic ideals in Western Europe differ markedly from the aesthetic vision of non-European societies in the same period, and even from later criteria of plastic beauty within Western Europe itself. The universality of art as a language is therefore obviously dependent on a knowledge of the historical and socio-cultural context in which each work of art is produced, or at least on one's willingness to temporarily suspend application of criteria conditioned by one's own background.

An even more serious source of difficulty is the fact that there are no identical definitions of art itself from one society to the other. What is considered in one place as a work of art may be perceived elsewhere essentially as a religious or cult object, while even within the confines of the same society, it is not always easy to draw a clear line between art and non-art. Where does art begin? Is not the purely utilitarian object which has been embellished through adjunction of decorative elements a work of art? Yet we have to concede that its primary objective is not aesthetic, and that the artistic dimension is secondary to its ultimate purpose. Must art then be defined only as that which has no immediate material use, as some authors have been inclined to do in the past? This would be an untenable position, for although artistic manifestations may be perceived as falling within a range of activities that may strictly be described as a non-utilitarian dimension of human existence, it would be an error to conclude that art has no direct connection with, or repercussion on, the material aspects of life. The influence of art is at once subtle and all-pervasive, since art is essentially a vehicle of communication in any society, in the sense that it serves to diffuse civilizing influences. Thus artistic endeavour not only belongs to the level of human activity connected with spiritual values, but is also an active component of social organization, hence of man's ability to influence and modify his environment. There can be no doubt that art as reflected in the songs, dances, music, decoration, sculpture painting,

Form and expression in African arts

myths, etc., of a given social group helps to define the culture of that group, and contributes to its sense of identity and its ability to function as a group.

Since it is essentially through social organization that man has been able to dominate nature, and art plays a vital role in helping to bind men together in organized social groups, it is from the point of view of its civilizing role that art is perhaps best defined. Thus art may be said to be the oldest and most eloquent testimony of man's social presence on earth. In any given age and society, the content and form of artistic endeavour is influenced by, and necessarily reflects, even if only by dialectical inversion, some of the beliefs, hopes, preoccupations and aspirations of that society and time, because art acts as a vehicle for social communication and cohesion. One may even go as far as to state that, although the civilization of any given social group encompasses divers aspects of sociological and cultural life, it is often art and allied cultural activities that carry the sharpest imprint of the peculiar genius of each family of humanity.

Thus, although for obvious reasons it is probable that no single definition of art would appear satisfactory to all persons, it may be said that the essential feature that characterizes art is that it is an instrument of social communication that utilizes harmonies and disharmonies in form, shape and sound to communicate emotions to the senses. More than that, art may be said to be a meditation about life, or rather a meditation that grows out of life, that proceeds directly or indirectly from the life experience. If we were to seek to express this idea differently, we might say that art is essentially an activity which seeks to take us deeper into the meaning of life, by reflecting in a realistic or in an abstract manner some of the abiding or transient aspects of our presence in the universe. In order to complete this definition, however, it is necessary to add that art is both form and content, and that the object of art is achieved as much through the agency of form and structure as through the actual content of such form. In other words, the meditative quality of a work of art may be reflected as much in the harmony or disharmony of its external forms as in the content that is communicated by the form, while an activity that may not necessarily have an aesthetic aim as its primary objective may be assimilated into the category of works of art because its forms reflect an artistic dimension. In other words, the work of art as *form* may serve as a vehicle for other types of social communication, as in the case of a poetic rendering of a religious message, or of a dance performed as part of a specific social rite.

The problems connected with the study of art are thus relatively complex. As Henri Focillon rightly points out in his now classical study *La Vie des Formes*:[1]

When it comes to interpreting a work of art, the problems to be faced are almost obsessively contradictory. Each work of art tends to be unique and to appear as a specific whole and as an absolute, yet at the same time, it belongs to a complex system of relationships. It is the result of independent activity, reflecting a free and superior dream, but also a convergence of the energies of civilizations.

The essential problem is that, although there are common denominators in art, even such a broad definition as we have offered in the preceding paragraphs does not entirely overcome the difficulty arising from the fact that no truly universal norms can be found for defining and categorizing art forms and content. Differences in cultural and sociological orientation and organization often make for enormous differences in modes of artistic expression, even within a single society. It is therefore necessary to study artistic manifestations within the framework of specific societies, as a preliminary to correlating art from different societies on a global level.

General characteristics of African art forms

The present work is an attempt to study traditional art forms in past and contemporary African societies from this point of view, and to suggest possible lines of thought for further study. Although it is necessarily brief in scope, it will seek to provide an introductory survey of African art forms and attempt to define their socio-cultural context in the short space available, albeit in a non-exhaustive manner. Our task is however rendered complex by the

1. Henri Focillon, *La Vie des Formes*, Paris, Presses Universitaires de France, 1964.

fact that, although it is fashionable to speak of 'African art'. 'African culture', 'African philosophy', etc., it would be an error to assume that African societies are homogeneous in nature, or that all African peoples share a common life experience. African art forms are by no means characterized by a unique style, and it would be an illusion to imagine that all art forms in Africa are identical in scope and orientation. All cultures are made up of a multiplicity of currents which may sometimes even appear antagonistic, and Africa is no exception to this general rule. The solution may therefore be to seek to classify African art on a regional basis for ease of reference. While one cannot subscribe to William Fagg's view that 'every [African] tribe is, from the point of view of art, a universe to itself',[1] it is obvious that he is on the right path when he chooses the tribe as a basic unit for the purpose of classification. However is that it must constantly be borne in mind that the tribe is not an impermeable universe that is exclusive of other similar units, and that, there may be a multiplicity of styles within a single tribal unit itself. In the end, William Fagg is forced to confess:

In a continent such as Africa, no tribe can be completely an island, for all must have relations with others. Such relations may or may not have visible effects upon a tribe's art. Many tribes have an effectively self-contained art which nevertheless forms a compromise or local fusion with one or other of the surrounding styles.[2]

What Fagg fails to add, however, is that there are also certain similar currents that have influenced various African tribes even though they may happen to be geographically very far apart. Thus although one must not oversimplify by postulating an absolute unity of art forms all over Africa, the tribal or regional unit must not be considered as an exclusive universe, either in the sense of being impermeable to the influence of other units, or even in the sense of reflecting the limits of a particular stylistic orientation.

Indeed, although there is no single African art form narrowly identifiable as African art to the exclusion of all others, there is a certain broad ensemble of styles and art forms, which together

1. William Fagg, *African Tribal Sculptures*, London, Methuen.
2. Fagg, op. cit.

constitute African art. Thus one can speak of African art both in terms of defining a geographical area in which certain works of art have originated, and in terms of a *number* of styles and techniques which are to be found within this geographical area. To argue, as Tibor Bodrogi[1] has done that there is no specific 'Africanness' in African art, and that no specific distinction can be made between African art and 'primitive' art from the rest of the world is fundamentally misleading. African art is the *totality* of art forms in Black Africa, which taken together or singly, are different from art forms in other parts of the world. For instance, there is no mistaking a *Bakongo* mask for a Japanese mask for *No* performances, or an Ife bronze with the work of Benvenuto Cellini. The fact that the Bakongo mask and the Ife bronze do not belong to an identical style does not mean that they cannot be distinguished from art forms of other parts of the world as being two African styles, amongst others. One might as well contend that because the *No* and *Bugaka* theatre techniques are different from each other, it is not possible to speak of Japanese theatre art as opposed to theatre forms in other parts of the world!

Not only are there often stylistic similarities between the art forms of different regional and tribal zones in Black Africa, but there are also a number of broad characteristics which transcend some of the differences between various styles. For instance, there are certain basic similarities in the relationship of art forms to a social and religious context, especially as it is possible to ascribe a similar background to most forms of ritual observances in nearly all African societies. In general, African art forms belong to an identical framework, even if this conceptual background exteriorizes itself in different ways.

One major characteristic common to all of Black Africa in the realm of sculpture is that carved masks are not made to be contemplated as works of art *per se*, but for use in connection with religious or social rituals or ceremonies. The artistic dimension here lies in the form, rather than in the basic aim and content, which have a religious or ritual goal. The two aspects cannot however be divorced from one another, and where attempts have been made to borrow

1. Tibor Bodrogi, *Art in Africa*, Budapest, 1969.

the technical accomplishments of form associated with African art (as with part of the Cubist experience) to the exclusion of the body of beliefs which made these forms acceptable within a social framework, the result has been a wholly abstract and intellectual art that in the end lacks the vitality and continuity of traditional African sculpture.

Another general characteristic of African art forms is that while dance (as in the ballet), spoken drama and concert music are generally practised as separate genres in the Western world, there is often no such distinction in the African context. Although there are instances of dance displays or music performances that are practised in isolation, music, dance and ritual are often linked in a single framework related to a specific religious or social ceremony. It is thus pertinent to consider them in their mutual relationship in seeking to analyse their aesthetic characteristics. For instance, masks used in such performances are not meant to be subjected to critical appreciation independently of a complex setting which includes other elements such as ritual and dance. Carved masks used for masquerade rituals must also be considered as part of a whole which includes dance, sculpture, music and ritual. As Leon Underwood[1] correctly stresses,

the mask in its African frame of dance and ceremony has not the same *separate* existence as the Italian Madonna surrounded by a gilded moulding. The African mask is not so detachable from its framework—the church in the case of the Italian Madonna. It is not an idol or identity of the deity but a carved representation or countenance; a focus of the broader effect in its elaborate framework of ritual, in which myth and belief are ceremoniously expressed in *music, dance, pageant, drama* and *sculpture*.

This does not mean that the artist who has carved the mask is not guided by formal considerations or does not strive for stylistic perfection. It means however that his artistry is not an end in itself, but a means to an end. The carved mask does not signify anything by itself, but because of, and in conjunction with, the context of beliefs

1. Leon Underwood, *Masks of West Africa*, London, Alec Tiranti, 1964.

Ola Balogun

and rituals to which it belongs, for the good reason that it is but one of many instruments in a coherent ensemble to which it contributes meaning and from which it derives significance.

A further characteristic of African art forms is the fact that they are seldom practised for entertainment value alone. Thus although entertainment aspects are often incorporated into art forms, they are generally not the most important aspects. For instance, in masquerade performances, the essential feature is the ritual function of the performance, but dance and sometimes mock pursuits of spectators by the masquerader provide entertaining features. Dance itself is seldom practised as pure entertainment, but on the occasion of specific festivities and rituals: nor are the dramatic aspects of ritual ceremonies—which are by definition not primarily for entertainment purposes—performed outside of the setting to which they belong. Perhaps the only major exception is the art of the story-teller or of the wandering minstrel, whose avowed purpose is to entertain an audience in exchange for remuneration. Even in this case, the stories or epic recitals often have as primary aim to provide moral lessons or useful knowledge of the past, rather than pure entertainment. It is however incorrect to postulate, as Elsy Leuzinger[1] has done, that '. . . religion is at the root of all African art'. This is certainly too wide a generalization.

In conclusion, one may say that certain characteristics are common to art forms in different parts of Africa, although it is by no means possible to speak of African art as a single homogeneous area of expression. From a stylistic point of view, African art may be said to incorporate a number of different styles, which, taken together or singly, are characteristic of Black Africa. The present study will therefore not only attempt to define and analyse the different art forms that are to be found in Africa, but also seek to present some of the stylistic characteristics that are to be found in African art forms, both on the basis of specific regions and of an ensemble of styles. We shall also envisage these art forms within the context of a conceptual framework common to the civilization of African peoples.

Art forms commonly encountered in African societies range

1. E. Leuzinger, *Afrique. Art des Peuples Noirs*, Paris, Albin Michel, 1962.

Form and expression in African arts

from sculptures (in wood, stone, iron, bronze, terracotta, etc.) to architecture, music, dance, ritual performances embodying dramatic elements, oral literature, etc. The range of artistic activity covers a wider spectrum among African peoples than is generally assumed, and is much more complex and diversified than ethnological studies have generally indicated.

As we have already pointed out, most of these art forms are not practised in isolation. For instance, oral literature, whether it be the epic recitals of court bards or the folktales by village storytellers, generally have a musical accompaniment which is often as important as the recital or story, while carved masks are often utilized in the course of ritual performances that also include song and dance. For the purpose of the present study however, we shall analyse these art forms singly as well as within the context of their overall setting.

PLASTIC ARTS

The mask as a work of art

Carving, whether in wood or in more durable materials such as stone, ivory or bone, is one of the mainstays of African art, and the medium through which African art has best come to be known outside Africa. Although a fair proportion of carving is done for ornamental purposes, as in head rests, nut bowls, pillar posts, etc., the most striking wood carvings are of masks designed for masquerade displays. Although some of them are the finest examples of African creative art, there has been much confusion about mask carvings, principally because of attempts to define them from Western European aesthetic perspectives. Such confusion is typified in the belief that African art is 'primitive', based on the assumption that it is because of inability to imitate nature that African sculptors have generally not attempted an exact copy of nature forms in the Graeco-Latin classical style, the corollary to this belief being the equally baseless assumption that mankind has evolved through the stage of 'clumsy' primitive art before finally achieving the formal perfection of Graeco-Latin art. The fallacy of this line of reasoning is however obvious, for there are two fundamental errors inherent in the point of view that it reflects. In the first place, aesthetic criteria are not necessarily similar the world over, and do not necessarily involve a direct imitation of nature forms. Cannot aesthetic appreciation rest as well on the *spiritual* dimension communicated by the art object rather than on its resemblance to nature, or its beauty or lack of beauty as a purely visual object? Secondly, there is no justification other than an ethnocentric vision of the world, for assuming that the lack of an aesthetic approach similar to that which has developed in Western Europe signifies an absence of formal perfection. Aesthetic appreciation of African art forms such as mask carvings by the indigenous African is fundamentally linked to an understanding of the purpose of the art object. Before discussing plastic factors in mask carvings as such, it is therefore necessary to analyse the general background and nature of African masquerades.

In most African societies, the religious life of the community is characterized by an active cult of spirit figures and gods, as well as by some forms of ancestor worship. Although there is general belief in the existence of a supreme being, God is almost everywhere considered as being too exalted and too distant to be directly concerned with human affairs. It is therefore to the multitude of lesser gods and deified ancestors that most Africans turn for intervention in their day-to-day affairs and for intercession with the forces of nature and the supreme being. Masquerade performances are generally part of ritual ceremonies designed to invoke such gods or to establish the communion of a community with them, as well as to remind members of the community of their relationship with non-human forces in the universe. The masquerade is therefore considered as a material manifestation of an intangible element, as a temporary incarnation of the non-human. Such a manifestation however requires human participation to make it possible, both on the level of a system of belief which renders it plausible, and on the level of a human agent (often the masquerader) who serves as a vehicle for the manifestation. Some sign or ensemble of signs must be found to distinguish this human agent from other human beings and establish the fact that for the duration of the rites he has ceased to be a human being and has become the avatar of the divinity or ancestor whose presence is being invoked. These signs, which have to be

Form and expression in African arts

accepted by the community as a whole as signifying such a change, include behaviour pattern (the masquerade behaves like the god and not like ordinary men), speech and utterances (the masquerade often utters weird sounds that are believed to be akin to sounds made by gods, or speaks in the manner of supernatural beings). The most important and most easily recognizable signs however lie in the costume. The costume suggests and imposes the presence of the divinity even to the most insensitive spectator. Such a costume often covers the masquerader from head to foot, but it might just as well involve a few lines of paint on the body or face of the masquerader. The function of the costume is essentially to *suggest*, to point to a reality beyond the physical presence of the human being who has donned it. It is above all a sign, in the same way as in theatre scenery a few branches may be used to suggest a forest in the action of a play. The costume, like the theatre prop, depends in part on convention, that is, an accepted significance codified by practice. But it may range from the subtle suggestion conveyed by a line of white paint on the body to the elaborate costume and mask that seek to reproduce the appearance of a specific animal or the imagined appearance of a supernatural being.

A frequent feature of the masquerade is the mask, which covers the face of the masquerader. This is by no means a compulsory feature, since the effect of dissimulating the human features and suggesting a different presence can also be achieved through covering the face with cloth or a thick veil or even by daubing paint on the face. In some cases, as in that of the devotee who is recognized as an avatar of a god through possession, the presence of the divinity is essentially established through the behaviour of the devotee, hence there is no need for a mask or face disguise. No hard-and-fast rule can be established for all African societies in this field, but in general, the costume of a masquerader serves to suggest a supernatural presence, and one of the most important elements in the costume is often the face or head mask.

Once the fundamental role of the mask (and the costume in general) in suggesting and establishing the presence of the supernatural is properly understood, it becomes possible to grasp the conceptual framework within which the carver of masks operates. The Western European artists who have been influenced by African

Ola Balogun

art apparently saw in the stylistic techniques of African mask and fetish carvers only an attempt to arrive at intellectual abstractions in viewing nature forms, and Cubism and other movements have therefore pursued this intellectually abstract approach to an extreme degree. This was however a mistaken interpretation, based on ignorance of the conceptual framework which dictated the styles employed by African mask carvers, who did not seek to achieve abstraction *a priori* as an intellectual interpretation of nature forms. This aspect no doubt exists, but is not the origin of mask forms. The masks are carved in the styles that can be observed because their form was designed to suggest and represent rather than portray. There is no need to be faithful to external forms either, because there is no tangible model from which the form could be copied (a god does not resemble anything that can be seen by man in normal life; his form may of course be imagined by the artist or seen in a vision or dream, but the artist cannot claim to be the only individual capable of reproducing the features of the god, or that his own version is necessarily the only accurate one, although convention in a community may fix certain general traits supposed to belong to a god). Even where the external form exists, it is a hidden essence of that form rather than its external appearance that the carver seeks to capture. The style of the mask carver is not merely a question of technique, but an approach imposed by the system of beliefs and the conceptual framework within which he operates.

This means that there has always been considerable scope for artistic freedom and improvisation within the larger framework of communal beliefs and conventions. For instance, if it is established that the divinity whose presence the mask is to help invoke is a frightening one, what is required of the artist is not a narrow copy of previous masks, but that he convey the idea of a frightening presence and suggest that presence in his work. He is frequently free to execute his own idea of what a frightening presence should look like, within the framework of local artistic canons and convention. There is also invariably an artistic tradition in which the artist is brought up that serves as a rather loose guideline. The basically suggestive nature of the work he is called upon to execute however protects the artist from being imprisoned in a narrow stylistic framework, for as long as he participates in the system of beliefs that he serves or at least understands the spirit of those beliefs, he can continue to evolve new forms to meet its needs and to find a flexible response to the problems of technique *per se*. The fundamental difference between the art of African carvers of cult masks and statues and the Western European abstract artist thus lies in the fact (stressed by Underwood) that

the belief, held commonly by the African carver and his tribe, made his abstractions significant and assured him of their acceptance by all, whereas the European artist lives in an objective world with no belief ruling enough to give direction of a commonly accepted significance to his abstractions. He is constrained therefore to make the attempt at *pure* abstractions which focus in the intellect, debarring them from having the same common appeal.[1]

Although it would be a mistake to consider them from the point of view of mere technique and plastic accomplishment, as we have already pointed out, there is no doubt that African mask carvings are a product of outstanding artistic skill and specialized technique. They reflect a careful and studied mastery of creative technique on many levels, and perhaps one of the most remarkable aspects of the creative skill of African mask carvers is the ability to achieve astonishing simplification of visual ideas originally derived from nature forms. The artist does not seek to copy nature, but he derives his inspiration from nature and goes on to create entirely new forms from this inspiration. It is in this direction that African art has most influenced contemporary abstract art in Western Europe.

In most mask carvings, it is as if the carver has sought to go beyond the mere outward appearance of nature forms to grasp their essence and proceed from there to new creative structures based on the perception of essence. If we take an example of one of the Bambara headpieces known as *Tyi-wara*, inspired by the form and grace of the antelope, we find that what remains of the antelope as a visual form has been reduced to a suggestion of the essential attributes of the animal, basically its sleek lines and grace, embellished by decorative flourishes. The beholder of the carving is carried beyond external form into the 'being' of the mythical animal which has been

1. Underwood, op. cit.

Ola Balogun

symbolized in essence by the form of the antelope. Or if we look at one of the Baoule masks from the Ivory Coast inspired by the human face, the basic heart form suggested by the line of the eyebrows through the cheeks to the chin is developed to its ultimate conclusion in one broad sweep which substitutes the heart form for the face.

The perceptive simplification of nature motives often leads the carver to develop a geometrical conceptualization of his source of inspiration. Thus the eyes become pure circles or squares or simple slanted lines, which are then spatially balanced against other features similarly conceived. The famous Basonge masks from the Congo basin represent one of the most remarkable developments of geometrical patterns inspired by the human face. Not only are the features themselves cast on a geometrical pattern of squares (for the eyes), but a collection of curved lines running across the entire surface in relief serves to accentuate the whole. This kind of geometrical play on form leads to the introduction of rhythmic elements in the plastic dimension, through the effects of symmetry and dissymmetry in the disposition of individual elements. In many Congolese and Gabonese masks for instance, the repetition of regular curves in the lines of facial features such as eyebrows, eyes and lips creates a pattern of rhythms reminiscent of musical rhythm.

Even more striking is the development of architectural patterns in many mask carvings. Even where the mask is made to be worn vertically over the face, it is rarely a flat surface, except perhaps in the case of some Bateke masks, of which a remarkable example is to be found in the Musée de l'Homme in Paris. Even in this case, the geometrical patterns and colours on the surface of the mask are so designed as to suggest depth: a slight relief is obtained by means of a straight line that runs across the middle of the mask, leaving the lower half of the mask recessed by about a quarter of an inch, while the upper half of the eye ovals are painted in a different colour from the lower half, suggesting depth. There is also a remarkable variety of Baoule masks known as *kple*, consisting of a flat disc, with only the eyes and sometimes the nose or lips offering a small relief. Most masks, however, go far beyond the suggestion of three-dimensional features and actually seek to achieve a three-dimensional scope. A remarkable example among face masks may be found in the Ekoi double-faced helmet masks, which reflect the

Form and expression in African arts

concept of a total space in which neither side can be described as the rear. The same theme is either repeated on the opposite side, or a complementary theme appears, with the result that the spectator is simultaneously in visual contact with both sides of the mask, so to speak. Even where there is only a front side in the face-mask, the surface of the mask is usually treated as an architectural rather than as a flat surface. Skilful use is made of relief to exploit formal themes and develop them to their logical conclusion, while the main carved area itself may be broken up into a series of architectural areas comprising multiple surfaces.

It is however in the case of head masks (i.e. designed to be worn horizontally on the head) that the fullest possible use can be made of three-dimensional space. We have already briefly described the famed Bambara *Tyi-wara* masks; other examples are to be found in the Baoule, Senufo (Ivory Coast) and Ijaw (southern Nigeria) headmasks, which represent buffalo spirits in the former case, and aquatic spirits in the latter. While the masquerade dances, the carving is presented to the spectators (depending on the masquerade's head), from different angles, making a different visual impact in each case. In effect, the mask's frontal aspect is entirely different from its sideways aspect, while the top of the mask can be seen to be on a different pattern when the masquerade dancer lowers his head. To illustrate this in practical terms, it would perhaps be appropriate to give an example in which the muzzle and teeth of the mythical creature are perceived as the most important part of the mask when it is viewed from in front, while the ears and the horns are the most striking features from the side view, and in the top view, the teeth and open muzzle disappear entirely, leaving a geometrical pattern built around the features of the face to strike the spectator.

One of the most outstanding examples of African carving combines the characteristics of the face mask and the head mask in the exploitation of three-dimensional space. These are the Gelede masks of the Yoruba (southern Nigeria), which in most cases cover both the face and the head. The face-mask part, for instance, might reflect a stylized (or naturalistic) representation of a human face, while the head and crown might be studded with three-dimensional figures represented in various activities, such as leopards, warriors, horses, rulers seated on thrones, etc. This part of the mask generally comprises a number of intricately carved elements, often representing a complex scene. Some recent versions of Gelede masks even comprise representations of motor vehicles and aeroplanes! The Senufo head-mask crests, comprising a variety of animal and divine figures carved on a hollowed out wooden panel surrounding an antelope head, are equally intricate.

The plastic genius of the African carver is often apparent in the decorative motives that accompany the main features of the carved mask. Generally, once the essential lines of the mask have been carved, it is embellished by various decorative designs, which vary from simple and subtle touches to the extreme baroque. In many cases, the decorative motives surround the main features and encase them, or are concentrated in a particular area such as the horns of animal figures, or the hair and beard (in carvings inspired by the human face). One might go so far as to say that it is in the area of decorative additions that the African carver seeks most to please the eye of the beholder. The most frequent decorative elements range from geometrical patterns to small leitmotifs repeated a number of times and to the addition of new and separate items to the original carving. In the latter case, for instance, a human figure might be surmounted by a bird figure or by some other external element introduced as a purely decorative addition.

Although African masks share many characteristics in common, certain stylistic traits are peculiar to specific regional or tribal zones. Thus while it would in the long run be erroneous to consider tribal demarcations as impermeable frontiers, as we have already pointed out, there is much to be gained in seeking to pinpoint the stylistic orientation that is peculiar to identifiable groups and subgroups. This is possible because in spite of discernible differences in inspiration, the overall stylistic traditions within a given tribal zone are often materialized in recognizable traits, although there are sometimes striking exceptions.

For instance, one of the most remarkable patterns of stylistic accomplishment in mask carvings is to be found among the Baoule of the Ivory Coast, among whom masks generally fall into two broad categories. In general, Baoule face masks portray human-like features in a naturalistic style that is visually very appealing, and which

Form and expression in African arts

combines a gentle, almost wistful touch with subtle stylization of the features. The natural proportions of the different parts of the human face are respected, while individual facial traits such as the eyes, the nose and the mouth are faithfully reproduced. The stylistic characteristic of Baoule face masks however lies in the treatment of the facial basin, which is generally a gently rounded heart-like surface. The cheek bones are dispensed with to further heighten the effect of tapering oval curves broken by the line of the nose in the centre. In keeping with the harmonious sweep of lines enclosing the facial basin, the lips appear as a small focal point at the bottom of the face. Characteristically, the lips are made to be rather smaller than their correct proportional relationship to the rest of the face, and are represented as being pursed, to accentuate the convergence of the sweeping curves that run from the eyebrows along the outer edge of the face. Seen from the side, the dominant impression is one of gently rounded curves, beginning with a sweeping forehead which appears to repose on a double convex line formed by the nose and the outer edge of the facial basin. The masks are generally surmounted by decorative figurines or animal figures or by simple decorative patterns woven into the outer surfaces of the mask across the head area. The abundance and interplay of such decorative elements permit vigorous affirmation of the personality and temperament of individual carvers.

The naturalistic trend of Baoule face masks in conjunction with the heart-like pattern of the inner face surface is also a frequent stylistic characteristic of face masks in certain Ibo and Ibibio carvings (Nigeria) and among some groups in the central African region, notably Fang, Bapunu and Balumbo. The style of these carvings however differs from the Baoule style in that, whereas the Baoule masks are usually monochromatic (blackened wood), masks from the above-mentioned regions display a marked difference between the face and head surfaces obtained by application of white kaolin on the face surface. Also, the face surface tends to be rounder and fuller, thus forming a circle rather than the elongated oval that is a characteristic feature of Baoule face masks. This effect is heightened by a marked reduction of the surface of the forehead, as well as by natural proportions in the lips and nose, and by establishing the chin as the lower point of the curved lines descending

Ola Balogun

from the eyebrows. Such masks are generally representations of female divinities or of female members of society, and are often surmounted by a thick crest reflecting hair style patterns.

The ultimate stylistic development of the basic heart form is to be found in some Bakwele masks, one of the most remarkable examples of which is at present part of the British Museum collection. In this case, there is little attempt at naturalistic representation of the human features. The mask appears as a perfect heart-shape set in a larger oval, broken in the middle by a long and very narrow triangular line. The whole effect is accentuated by a deliberate insistence on the opposition between the heart-like excavation that forms the main facial surface, and the slightly concave surface of the outer oval, with the lips appearing as a curved single line at the bottom of the heart shape. An even more striking example of extreme stylization of a heart-form face shape can be found in some Pangwe masks from Gabon. Here, the face surface is treated as two oval lobes which meet in a depression in the centre at the touching point of the eyebrows, with a long straight line materialized by the nose running down the middle and forming the separation between the two lobes. The effect produced by the sweeping contour thus formed is accentuated by the fact that the entire face surface is painted in white, while the contour line of the heart shape, including the nose-line running down the centre, is stressed in black. In addition, the contour line is already in slight relief, so that the total effect is of utter sobriety within a forceful plastic effect.

While most masks utilized for masquerade displays cover the face only, and are completed by either a raffia or cloth adjunct that covers the rest of the head, the helmet mask, which is worn over the whole of the face and head, occupies a total three-dimensional space. Since they have to be large enough for the head of the masquerade dancer to fit inside, helmet masks tend to be rather massive. The bulk in size, as well as the fact that the helmet-mask must be conceived in such a way as to be viewed from any angle and still remain visually intelligible, generally excludes plastic abstractions of the type commonly found in face masks. Thus the Ekoi type of helmet mask (from south-eastern Nigeria) which is frequently Janus-faced, is often naturalistic in its portrayal of human features. In striving for a natural effect, the carvers of these masks generally go

Form and expression in African arts

as far as to cover the whole surface with finely cured antelope skin to create the illusion of human-type skin, while stones or bone chips are inlaid into the mask to represent eyes and teeth. The helmet masks of the Mendi of Sierra Leone (utilized for Bundu society dances) are totally different; they are carved in a squat conical form tapering at the top into an elaborate head style. The face surface is often set into a small frontal part of the mask which is dominated by a broad tapering forehead, thus placing the accent on the head as a volume that dominates all else. Skilful decorative designs, which may even form entire strips running across the whole surface of the mask, also serve to highlight the total effect achieved by the massive volume of the head mask.

For sheer plastic audacity, some of the African masks are hardly to be surpassed. One remarkable use of an architectural conceptualization of space is to be found in a Bacham mask from the United Republic of Cameroon which is at present in the Musée Reitberg in Zurich. In this carving, which is based on a highly stylized representation of the human features, the cheek bones have become protruding conical structures with a gently rounded top, on which the eyes rest in a horizontal plane, while the sockets beneath the eyebrows have become elongated vertical surfaces towering above the eyes, rather like the upper lid of an oyster shell within which the eye reposes. This remarkably audacious treatment of surfaces (it is under the influence of styles of this type that the cubist movement originated) is inconceivable in the absence of very advanced plastic concepts. The art of the carver reveals itself in the total mastery of spatial and plastic factors in one dynamic whole. In a sense, the effect is to isolate the mask in a time-space continuum of its own, for it becomes a frozen moment in eternity, yet the movements of the masquerade lend it a new life and plunge it into the rhythms of human life. As the masquerade dances, it is that frozen moment of eternity grasped by the carver's art that is set in motion to the rhythm of music, stimulating the emotional perception of the spectator both by its plastic rhythm in the isolated space of the carving itself, and in a larger rhythm linked to dance movements within the space occupied by the mask and the onlooker. When this is added to the emotional impact of the socio-cultural significance of the dance ritual, the cumulative effect is one of intense participation,

Ola Balogun

leading to final catharsis through the combination of emotional stimulus and participatory action.

The skilful use of paint to highlight certain plastic aspects and contribute to the overall plastic effect is also as an important factor in mask carving. Since the mask is not designed to be contemplated in a static pose, it is generally so conceived that its component elements stand out even in motion. Coloured paint is therefore often applied to deepen the three-dimensional effect achieved by the mask, and to accentuate the global plastic impression created by the dance movements of the masquerade. The total effect is therefore one of a moving sculpture unravelling strips of colour and mass as it dances in rhythm to music and runs to and fro across the visual field covered by the onlooker, with the patches of colour being provided by the costume of the masquerade and the strokes of paint on the mask surface. Symmetry or dissymmetry of forms on the carved surface is also accentuated by paint or other colouring, which serves to break up architectural surfaces in some cases, or to create a new decorative dimension in addition to carved decoration. Very skilful use is also made of beads, corals, cowries and pieces of glass in decorating carved masks. No piece of material is considered too lowly for such use, provided it can produce a pleasing effect on the eye.

On the whole, African mask carvings are striking for the dynamic and imaginative use of rhythmic and abstract elements to produce a cumulative plastic effect. They offer some of the most interesting examples of mastery of plastic forms by the African artist, and even though, as we have seen, they are not primarily designed to produce an aesthetic effect as such, they achieve this end as well as the goal of arousing the emotions of the spectator through a variety of means other than the creation of a mere pleasing form. The mask is above all a sign, a symbol, and the artist's aesthetic preoccupations must therefore be secondary to the ritual role which the mask is supposed to fulfill, yet this very factor is what gives him almost total liberty as regards the plastic solutions he employs. By a strange paradox, it is precisely because the object to be served by the mask must take precedence over his private vision as an artist that he achieves total artistic liberty in his treatment of form, since the aim of his work is most often to suggest immaterial forms, rather

Form and expression in African arts

than copy nature directly. Form and content are intimately linked in an organic whole, yet independent of each other in any narrow didactic sense. The form is a window to the content in so far as it suggests the presence of a spiritual content by providing a material crucible for the imagination to develop in, but the form never really sets out to be the direct reflection of that content. Like the name of an individual, the outward form of a mask represents in an abstract sense, and the specific plastic technique employed thus emerges as a means to an end, and not an end in itself. It is for this reason that an ensemble of different styles may be used simultaneously in a non-exclusive sense to achieve an identical end, which is to suggest the presence of a higher spiritual reality through the intermediary of the mask.

Decorative carvings

The decorative mastery we have noticed in the carved mask is even more pronounced in the purely decorative objects for domestic use. Here is one instance where the whole aim is to please the eye, or amuse the beholder, or simply hold his attention. Thus many small pieces of domestic furniture are embellished by adjunction of decorative elements, which may range from abstract geometric patterns to carved figures or other full-scale additions. The field of application ranges from royal thrones to headrests, door surfaces, pillar posts, wooden containers, etc. Rarely is any surface that can be embellished by decorative carving left bare. One of the most striking examples in this field are the doorposts used in architecture in most parts of Africa. Among the Yoruba, for instance, the decorative embellishment of doorposts and wooden pillars has been carried to great lengths, and may depict a mounted horseman or a standing or kneeling figure carved in a style perhaps best described as naturalistic abstraction. Often, the figure itself is naturalistic, but the representation of some essential attribute is simultaneously an abstract interpretation of its fundamental nature and relationship to the whole. For instance, a figure mounted on horseback may be depicted in realistic proportions, while the horse itself is shown on a very small scale, even though none of its features are omitted. Again, skilful use of paint often underscores the desired effect,

Ola Balogun

while the merging of abstract geometrical patterns and external representational forms strikes an interesting plastic balance. Favourite motives include animals and humans.

Decorative carving on door surfaces or on wooden panels is of particular interest, especially if it is borne in mind that pictorial art on canvas or silk frames has never developed in Africa, as in the Far East and in the Western world. Carved decorations on wooden panels are therefore often the nearest equivalent to painting as practised in other societies. It is of interest to note that representation of perspective is deemed unnecessary, and that the carved surface is treated as two-dimensional from this point of view, with no attempt to create the illusion of a third dimension through added perspective. Sometimes, the carved panel tells a story rather in the same manner as the modern cartoon strip, with scenes running through several successive horizontal lines. Beginning from the top, for instance, the carver might depict a group of warriors taking leave of a king, followed by another scene of preparation for battle, then of the warriors travelling on horseback towards their destination, followed by a battle scene, then by the triumphant return of the warriors with booty and captives which they present to the king, and finally by a scene of popular rejoicing. The treatment of space in these carvings often reflects a totally abstract conceptualization of space-time categories. Moments in time are depicted in successive fashion, but linear space is treated on a single plane, with both elements being combined in a single story representation.

Wood sculpture

As in the case of masks carvings, African sculpture is mainly in wood. Ivory has been used in some instances, as well as certain types of stone, although the use of stone for sculpture is infrequent. In most cases where stone sculptures are found, a soft type of stone known as soapstone, which has similar characteristics to wood, is utilized. Harder stones such as quartz and granite have also been utilized in some rare cases, as at Ife in western Nigeria.

In order to be able to understand the stylistic characteristics of African sculpture, it is necessary to discuss the uses to which sculpture is applied among African peoples. As with masks, it is

Form and expression in African arts

necessary to stress from the outset that we are not dealing with objects conceived for aesthetic purposes as such, and designed for display with this perspective in view. Most African sculptures are power objects or symbolical substitutes for ancestors and gods, and are therefore primarily aimed at fulfilling a function in this connection. It is often evident that the sculptor's stylistic pre-occupations are closely linked with the object to be fulfilled by the sculpture, as well as by already existing plastic traditions. There is hardly ever any attempt to reproduce natural traits or to base sculpture on realism. It is therefore rare to find any life-size statues or even small-size statues based on real-life proportions. There is no doubt that the need for the sculptor to concede foremost importance to the purpose to be served by his work is a determining factor in the conceptionalization of most African sculptures, rather than *a priori* consideration of effects pleasing to the eye of the beholder. This does not however mean the absence of search for plastic perfection and harmony (or deliberate disharmony). On the contrary, because the African sculptor cannot in most cases rely on the facility of obtaining acceptance of his work through recognition of resemblance with known nature models, he is obliged to place greater stress on plastic accomplishment, as opposed to realism. There is no doubt that some of the most remarkable achievements of African sculpture can be traced to the important role of non-realistic conceptualization in the quest for plastic harmony. Being relieved of the obligation to copy directly the outward manifestations of nature means that the African sculptor in the traditional setting has had to devote much thought to the ways of achieving purely plastic perfection in his work, hence the extraordinary quality of artistry that is often displayed in such work. By what might appear a paradox in Western eyes, it is precisely because the African sculptor has not conceived his work exclusively in terms of creation of forms pleasing to the eye that such sculptures achieve startling visual effects.

There has been considerable controversy as to the significance that should be attached to the uses to which African sculpture is put. Some sources have attempted to define sculpture in the African context as strictly utilitarian, while others see the magico-religious dimension as all-embracing. The reality of the situation is however

Ola Balogun

far more complex than either of these generalizations indicates, for it is obvious that both the utilitarian and the magico-religious dimensions are part of an all-embracing sculptural mould.

One of the best-known categories of sculpture are commemorative statuettes of ancestor-figures, and ritual statuettes of gods that are placed in religious shrines to represent divinities or devotees of the gods to whom such shrines are dedicated. These statuettes are conceived basically to serve a religious function, hence a conceptualization that relies heavily on symbols and emblems of the essential attributes associated with the god or ancestor figure. The magico-religious function is a fundamental factor in the case of these statuettes, as with other types of carvings used for religious purposes. Such sculptures are above all 'power objects', and their efficacity in the religious sphere is as much dependent on the sculptor's skill in the first instance as on the rites associated with them. A clumsily executed work or one that falls too far outside the traditional canons of style peculiar to the tribal or regional zone within which it is created would not be acceptable in so far as it fails to fulfil normal expectations. The sculpture and its characteristics are therefore closely dependent on the socio-cultural context in which it is created, from the point of view of both inspiration and perception by a viewing public. It is for this reason that attempts to encourage production of such art works on a commercial scale with a view to restituting mere outward characteristics of style are inevitably doomed to failure. The stylistic features of sacred sculpture and the technical responses they embody to purely artistic problems and preoccupations are merely part of a much wider totality that embraces a system of beliefs extending beyond the artist as an individual. In this sense, one may go as far as to postulate that such sculpture is the collective work of a civilization, accomplished through the agency of the artist performing the role of a medium for the materialization of collective belief and vision. The sculptor's originality and individual skill expresses itself in this context through his ability to achieve perfect rendering of the 'power' characteristics of the sculpture he has been asked to execute, and through a harmonious blend of artistic finish and decorative embellishment.

This basic orientation extends beyond sculptures made for

Form and expression in African arts

purely religious purposes, and is similarly present in sculptures connected with social and cultural customs. One striking example that helps illustrate this are the twin dolls (*ibeji*) carved among the Yoruba of Nigeria in honour of twins, and the *akua ba* dolls of the Ashanti of Ghana. The Yoruba *ibeji* dolls are conceived to serve as a kind of substitute for real-life twins born into a family. The dolls are used to 'fix' the spirit of the twins on a spiritual level, and should one of them die in childhood, the doll substitute is 'brought up' with the surviving twin, receiving food and clothes in place of the dead twin. The *ibeji* dolls are used both for rites connected with the divinity associated with twin births, and for the purely socio-psychological function of providing a 'substitute' for the twins. *Ibeji* statuettes are carved in characteristic fashion and bear no resemblance to the actual twins, since the sculptor never attempts to use the real-life twins as his model. Instead, he seeks to be faithful to the traditional Yoruba pattern of *ibeji* sculpture, itself the outcome of a process of collective acceptance of the ideal representation of twin children. Thus an *ibeji* sculpture is immediately recognizable for what it is in any part of Yorubaland, yet the artist has scope to express his own individuality and skill through variations in decorative patterns, as well as through the degree of perfection displayed in his execution of the established model. The *akua ba* dolls of the Ashanti, which have even less of a ritual function than *ibeji* dolls, display the same marked fidelity to an established model. The basic pattern of the *akua ba* doll is a flat disc-shaped head set on a narrow cylindrical body traversed horizontally by projecting arms. All *akua-ba* dolls, designed primarily for toys for little girls, are variations on this basic model, said to embody a concep-tualization of the Ashanti ideal of beauty. Here again, the basic stylistic framework within which the sculptor operates is derived from a socio-cultural heritage, from which it cannot be arbitrarily divorced. It is the sentiment of continuity with a commonly shared heritage that determines the sculptor's technique, rather than a mechanical reproduction of the stylistic characteristics of previous work. The distinction is crucial, for it is important to understand that the sculptor does not merely copy the details of traditional patterns of sculpture, but uses the accepted traditional model as an inspirational guide from which his own creative skill blossoms.

Mechanical copies for the purely commercial purpose of satisfying tourist demand remain lifeless and artistically sterile, while work that has its roots in the perspective of socio-cultural continuity outlined above is as vigorous as past works from the point of view of artistic execution.

Even where the purpose of sculpture is to preserve the memory of outstanding figures in society such as kings, as illustrated by the commemorative statues of Bakuba kings, the stylistic characteristics are determined above all by the established pattern for such sculptures. The king is shown in the same invariable sitting posture, and each king is identifiable not from facial traits, which are virtually identical in all, but from the attributes characteristic of his reign which he is holding. For instance, King Shamba Bolongongo is seen seated in front of an African draught-board, holding a knife (symbolical of peace), and is thus characterized by allusion to his favourite game, and by evocation of the fact that peace lasted for so long in his reign that war weapons were replaced by knives for hunting and domestic occupations. The individuality of each king is expressed without the sculptor having to represent his features as a distinguishing element, while the continuity of the institution of kingship is stressed by the basic similarity of each sculpture.

Although they are based on rather similar artistic traditions, sculptures differ from masks for a number of reasons. Whereas the mask reproduces only the face or at most the head, the sculpture is often devoted to a physical representation of the various parts of the body, including the torso. The approach to signifying essential attributes or reflecting such attributes by 'symbolical shorthand' is therefore necessarily different. The mask is part of a masquerade costume that forms a significant whole, while the sculpture itself is a whole. Sculptures may therefore be said to follow an entirely different line of development in many respects, for the simple reason that there is a vast difference in volume in space, contrary to face masks which occupy only a half volume as it were, the other half of the volumetric space being taken up by the cloth or raffia part of the costume that envelops the head. In sculpture, therefore, volumes and surfaces have to be treated within the context of an all-encompassing space, whereas masks deal merely with a single vertical plane.

Form and expression in African arts

In order to best understand these differences, it is most instructive to examine instances in which the sculpture appears as an adjunct to the face-mask, as in cases in which face-masks are surmounted by sculptures representing human or animal figures. The contrast in style is striking. Whereas the face-mask is conceptualized within the framework of a single horizontal plane, with a marked tendency towards abstraction, the sculptured figure that surmounts it immediately strikes the beholder as less abstract, even though it is never actually realistic, except in the case of animal and bird figures. The sculpture may be said to materialize what the figure represents in more concrete terms than the mask, which is only part of a costume designed to suggest the presence of the supernatural when worn by a masquerader in conjunction with the appropriate ritual performance. To summarize the difference, we might say that the mask suggests, while the sculpture is a physical substitute for what represents, thus necessitating a radically different treatment of themes. Symbolization in the sculpture is often obtained through attributive traits, whereas the face-mask has to place its 'symbolic shorthand' in the form itself.

The considerations outlined above explain the difference in treatment of the face surface even where the sculpture represents the head of the subject, as in the case of the *Obom* masquerade headpiece among the Ekoi of Nigeria, which is essentially an anthropomorphic head sculpture carried on the crown of the head by the masquerade. However, in the case of head-masks inspired by buffalo or fish themes, there is a tendency towards abstractive stylization within the total form, because we are really confronted with a face-mask that lies on a horizontal instead of a vertical plane. This is particularly striking in Senufo head-masks from the Ivory Coast, which are often a stylized representation of crocodile-buffalo features, involving a thematic opposition between the streamlined curves of the face surface and of the horns and the square, jagged projection of the teeth and jaws. A striking illustration of the abstractive freedom achieved through such treatment is a remarkable Senufo head-mask in the Abidjan Museum; this bewildering construction suggests movement through a streamlined forward flow of face elements on the horizontal plane, while the volumetric mass, abundantly decorated by several pairs of horns that break the suggested forward flow, simultaneously imposes a strong element of stability. The shark-inspired head-masks of the Kalabari and other Ijaw peoples of the Niger delta area show an even more interesting tendency towards abstract streamlining of essential physical traits. In this case, volumetric development is played down in favour of stylized conceptualization on the horizontal plane.

One striking example of total abstraction in a horizontal sculpture surmounting a mask is the *kanaga* mask of the Dogon of Mali, which is made up of a flat vertical element in the centre crossed by two flat horizontal pieces near the top and the bottom; this has sometimes been described as an extreme stylization of the human form. The *kanaga* mask has in fact many different levels of meaning, depending on the degree of initiation of the beholder, one of the ultimate of these being that it is a representation of the Supreme Being *Amma*, pointing with his hands and feet towards heaven and earth. Similarly, a taller form of flat vertical sculpture (known as *sirige*) on the same type of Dogon masks is said to symbolize the house inhabited by the first eighty human ancestors. The *kanaga* and *sirige* are however more properly to be seen as symbolical abstractions, rather than as sculptures designed to occupy a volume in space.

The significant factor about African sculpture in general is that the statuette of a god-figure or animal is generally not conceived as a visual representation of the original object, but as a substitute for it, or a form of magic evocation of it, hence the accent on symbolization of essential traits, rather than on factual representation as such. This explains some of the recurring themes, such as prominent sex organs symbolizing fertility functions, or woman-child figures with the mother shown giving suck to her child. In anthropomorphic figures, the head is often on a larger scale in proportion to the rest of the body. Where two figures of unequal social importance feature in a sculpture a frequent device is to reflect the difference in social status through a sharp variation in proportion. Thus a king shown with an attendant by his side is generally much larger in proportion than the attendant. This tendency is particularly pronounced in Yoruba sculpture, the typical example being that of mounted horsemen whose heads are deliberately made larger in proportion to their torsos and limbs, while the horses are of greatly reduced proportion within the total ensemble.

The treatment of volumes in African sculpture is also closely related to the fact that the sculptor usually executes his sculptures by whittling down a single piece of wood, a factor that tends to impose continuity between different volumetric planes. There is also scarcely ever any attempt to show a figure in movement or involved in some form of physical activity such as might distract from the volumetric balance of the sculpture. The elimination of tension in terms of physical posture ensures that there is no interference with overall plastic harmony in the structural sense.

The treatment of emblems and symbols associated with ancestor and god-figures in sculpture shows the extraordinary liberty that the African artist manages to preserve within strictly defined conventions. Some of the sculptures of statuettes associated with the worship of the Yoruba thunder divinity Shango are a perfect illustration of the development of emblematic themes as the most significant part of the sculptured subject. Sculptures in Shango shrines often depict priests or devotees of his cult, whose association with Shango is shown by the two characteristic symbols of his cult in their hands, the double-headed axe (*oshe*) and a calabash rattle (*sere*). In a parallel development, the priest or devotee may himself feature as part of a carving of the double-headed axe, with the trunk of his body forming the handle while his head appears as the central portion of the axe-head! Thus by an astonishing reversal of metaphor, the symbol has been carried to its extreme logical development by incorporating that which it originally served to identify, in what may be called the embodiment of a pure idea. The symbol not only serves to identify, but can also incorporate, or be incorporated into, the sculptural object in a perfect symbiosis rendered possible by its role as an abstraction. To ponder on this development enables us to understand that all sculptural undertaking in the traditional African context lies in the realm of abstraction, not so much as a response to purely plastic problems (in the sense associated with the abstract dimension of Cubist sculpture, for instance), but because the sculpture itself originates as an abstraction, a materialized manifestation of idea-essence. This abiding trait is common to virtually all African sculpture.

Ola Balogun

Thus the *tyi wara* sculptural headpieces of the Bambara masquerades express the idea of movement and grace in the antelope, and not its reality as such, hence the extreme stylization employed to signify and symbolize the perceived attributes. The logical prolongation of such development, as we have seen, is the emergence of the symbol as a sign that communicates an abstract concept or idea, as in the case of the Dogon *kanaga* and *sirige* masks, which are surmounted by an abstract symbolic sculptural piece, or the famous Bobo masks which are surmounted by a carved vertical headpiece on which the interplay of geometric patterns and designs embodies esoteric symbols whose deep significance can only be perceived by the initiated.

A different form of symbolism may be found in the attitudes of sculptural figures, as exemplified in the *nomo* sculptures among the Dogon, who are believed to have emigrated from the Manding aree in Guinea to their present abode on the rocky hilltops between Bandiagara and Hombori in Mali. They are thought to have inherited the *nomo* sculptures from an ancient cave-dwelling population known as the Tellem; these sculptures generally represent an ancestor with upraised hands in a characteristic ritual gesture.

In some cases, symbolical abstraction is embodied in the form of the sculpture, especially in sculptures which are analogous to masks in developing on a vertical plane, as in the case of the *akua ba* dolls of the Ashanti, or the *Mbulu Ngulu* sculptures of the Bakota of Gabon, which like the *akua ba* dolls consist of a representation of a flattened figure in which the face surface is the dominant feature. The typical Bakota reliquary figure consists of a large oval face mounted on a thin short stalk, the original wood being covered over by a thin copper plate, and it is surmounted by a crescent like headpiece from which two oval side pieces seem to flow. The face is often set in a concave depression, and some of these sculptures are double-faced, being known as *Mbulu-viti* in such cases.

In general, African sculpture, whether conceived for religious or other purposes, may be said to proceed from a conceptual form of realism, rather than from visual realism. In other words, it is a realism that does not seek to reproduce outward traits faithfully, but which is preoccupied with producing an acceptable substitute for the original object or figure by means of symbolical or attributive

Form and expression in African arts

identity. Physical details of the original are thus only relevant to the extent to which they signify attributive features, as distinct from a realistic reflection of its total physical presence, as might be sought in an artistic tradition of portraiture, for instance.

Perhaps the most astonishing aspect of African sculpture in relation to objects used for sacred or ritual purposes, is that the sculpture is developed as a power object through concentration of form, for it is as much the achievement of form as the power of ritual which imprisons in the statuette the forces whose intervention is sought. The power of sculpture to serve as a vehicle for supernatural forces is at the origin of the sculptor's quest for perfection. Like words, objects have ultimately the power to transform life. Form has a life and force of its own, and the artist in his dialogue with form must take cognizance of this important fact, if he is not to harm himself or create a malfunction of the forces for which his sculpture is to serve as a conduct. This is perhaps the origin of the esoteric function attached to certain forms, and it is against this background of a total purpose of art that the sculptor works. On the ultimate level, art is a prolongation of life because it is imbued with a life of its own; the form of the man-made object becomes a substitute for the supernatural or human because it has significance in the same way as a name has, and because it captures and imprisons a part of the original through symbolical identity.

Stone sculptures

Stone sculptures in soft stone, known as soapstone, generally bear close stylistic resemblance to wood sculptures, no doubt a result of the similarity between the two materials for the practical purpose of sculpture. Numerous examples of small statuettes made from soapstone have been found in the region of Esie, in the west of Nigeria, and in the Kissi and Sherbro areas of present-day Sierra Leone, where these statuettes are known as *pomdo* and *nomoli*. Small stone figures known as *mintadi* have also been found among the Bakongo of present-day Zaire. However, although the carving techniques utilized in these figures are similar to wood carving techniques, they tend to be more naturalistic in style than the typical wood sculptures of the Bakongo.

Ola Balogun

Stone sculptures in hard materials, such as quartz and granite, show greater differences in the styles and techniques from wood sculptures. Perhaps the most remarkable examples of these stone sculptures are to be found in the Yoruba spiritual capital of Ile-Ife, in Nigeria, where elaborately carved ritual objects and astonishingly sensitive human and animal figures have been recovered in some of the city's sacred groves. In style and execution, these sculptures reflect a high degree of artistic mastery, in view of the difficulty involved in working in such hard material. An even more remarkable style of sculpture is reflected in the famous stone sculptures discovered in the Ikom area in the vicinity of Nigeria's Cross River. Carved in hard basalt stone, these sculptures, which are believed to be in commemoration of past clan heads, are derived by engraving intricate patterns on the surface of cylindrical boulders. The engraved patterns generally indicate facial traits and a protruding navel, with decorative motives surrounding and flowing from the face and the main area of the trunk. No attempt is made to carve the limbs or even indicate their presence, and the sculpted figure generally appears as a trunk growing out of the ground. The head is sometimes delineated from the trunk in these powerfully suggestive statues that radiate a deep impression of awe and serenity. The Ikom stone sculptures are virtually the only example of life-size sculpture in Black Africa.

Terracotta sculpture

Terracotta seems to have been one of the earliest and mostly widely used materials for sculpture among African peoples. Unlike wood, it has been rather well preserved over the ages, and specimens have been found dating well over 2,000 years, notably from the Sao civilization of the Lake Chad area and the Nok culture of central Nigeria. The Nok terracottas, which reflect a considerable degree of technical mastery, are among the most refined terracotta sculptures that exist in Africa. It is perhaps necessary to point out at this stage that the very nature of technique in terracotta sculpture necessarily influences the sculptor's stylistic approach, as compared to wood carving. In wood carving, the sculptor's approach is substractive, since form is achieved by progressively chipping away

Form and expression in African arts

the surface of the wood until the desired traits appear, while in terracotta, which is obtained by moulding wet clay and firing it at a high temperature to produce hardness, the form is pressed into shape by gentle strokes of the fingers. Whereas wood sculptures tend to deal with forms on the level of volumes and planes, terracotta bronze and iron sculptures do not lend themselves to the same kind of stylistic approach; rather, the forms are treated as a single surface in which there is no differentiation between various planes. Terracotta seems to lend itself best to rounded forms, and some of the Nok terracottas boldly explore basic forms, such as the cone, the cylinder and the sphere, in sculptures of the human head, encompassing the flow of form within the chosen shape. The Nok terracotta sculptures, which belong to a civilization that disappeared so long ago that it is not possible to find out who the creators of the Nok style of sculpture were, are thought to have some affinity with later sculptures in terracotta and bronze further south in Ile-Ife, a spiritual centre of Yorubaland. The style of Nok sculpture is however unique, and several distinct features of this style are worthy of mention. Although the Nok terracottas visibly reproduce human features, the style may be said to be more of an expressionist than of a naturalist content. The eyes are often dominant features, appearing as large concave semi-circular ovals set in symmetrical opposition to the total face area. In some other sculptures, it is the lips that play the role of a raised and structurally dominant area in opposition to the rest of the face.

The expressionism of the Nok sculptures gives way to a marked naturalistic flow of features in the less well-known terracotta sculptures from Krinjabo in the lower Ivory Coast. It is however in the famed terracotta heads from Ife that a naturalistic flow achieves full development. The Ife terracotta sculptures, like the bronze sculptures from the same city, are believed to be commemorative effigies of early rulers of the city, and of members of the royal family. Remarkably serene and life-like in appearance, these terracottas and bronzes are so far removed from all other currents of African sculptural style that they seem to form an enigma. Some anthropologists, like the German Frobenius, have even gone as far as to speculate on the possibility of Greek influence on Ife sculpture. Such speculation however fails to recognize that even in the

Ola Balogun

pursuit of a naturalistic orientation, the Ife style is still radically distinct from non-African styles of sculpture, and possesses a specific personality of its own. The main explanation for the difference between the Ife style and other stylistic traditions in Africa lies perhaps in the fact that Ife art was almost exclusively dependent on royal patronage, and that the life-like portrayal of royal figures was certainly a court institution introduced and maintained by the early ruling dynasties. The figures are very life-like, yet betray a form of idealization tending towards perfection of features.

Bronze casting

Bronze was introduced to Africa at a later period than iron, and the impact of bronze-casting in Africa has therefore largely been on sculpture, rather than on tool and weapon-making, as in some other parts of the world. In the principal African centres where it was practised, bronze-casting was carried out by the *cire perdue* method, in which basic modelling is done on a clay core, over which is applied a wax coat on which the sculptor imprints the finer modelling details. A second layer of clay several inches thick is then applied over the wax, and when the clay has hardened sufficiently, the model is heated to make the wax melt, leaving a space in between the two layers of clay into which the molten bronze is poured through runners attached to the top of the model.

The Ife bronzes, like the terracottas, are a court-inspired art almost exclusively devoted to commemorative effigies of past Ife rulers and heroes. Most of the kings are shown wearing a royal diadem adorned at the centre with an emblem similar to the Egyptian Uraeus. In most of the heads, small holes have been bored around the mouth and across the top of the forehead, presumably for receiving real hair. The faces of some of the heads are covered by fine vertical lines, but it is difficult to tell whether this is a representation of a type of facial marking common in the royal family or whether it was originally conceived as a decorative feature of the bronzes. The heads are both naturalistic and idealized, with a marked tendency to portray the features in perfect light, without any of the blemishes associated with age or physical imperfection. Where the heads are crowned with the diadem or with other forms

Form and expression in African arts

of headwear, a wealth of detail is generally shown in the treatment of the headpiece. A small number of Ife bronzes are figurines of exquisitely rendered proportions, usually depicting royalty, as in the famous casting of an Ife king in full regalia with his left leg intertwined with the right leg of his consort, who appears at his side (Ife Museum). There are also some remarkable examples of ceremonial stools cast in bronze, characterized by a profusion of symbolic and decorative details and figures that blend perfectly however into a single harmoniously controlled form, which is that of the stool itself.

The bronze-casting traditions of the Benin kingdom, some 200 miles to the east of Ife, are said to have been introduced from Ife during the reign of King Oguola. Some of the Benin bronzes, like their Ife counterpart, are naturalistic effigies of rulers, which however display less idealized features than the Ife bronzes. The Benin heads generally have a circular hole in the crown of the head in which an elephant tusk is believed to have been fitted originally. The treatment of coral bead crowns worn by the kings and of the coral headgear of the queens inclines more towards decorative patterning than the careful reproduction of detail evident in the Ife bronzes, announcing the baroque profusion of decorative and symbolic elements characteristic of later Benin bronzes. In some of these, the bronze head is overlaid with numerous totemic animals and decorative outgrowths, culminating in an amazingly vigorous portrayal. Benin bronze casting also offers many examples of finely accomplished figures and figurines depicting court messengers, warriors and noblemen, as well as foreign visitors, such as Portuguese soldiers; in all of them there is a marked attention to expressive as opposed to attributive details, especially in the treatment of proportions, particularly of the limbs in relation to the body. Perhaps one of the most outstanding of these figures is that depicting a nobleman warrior on horseback (Lagos Museum), remarkable for the precision and vigour with which the details of his armour, weapons and horse harness are treated. At the Benin royal court, bronze-casting was also utilized in making bronze plaques on which subjects stood out in relief; these reveal surpassing artistic skill which is sometimes unfortunately overshadowed by excessive baroque ornamental outgrowth. Perhaps the purest and most serene form of Benin sculpture is to be found in the small sculptured pendants in bronze, ivory or gold, usually in the form of masks depicting a ruler in highly naturalistic style reminiscent of the Ife style, which are worn by Benin kings during certain ceremonies. The outer fringes of these mask-like pendants are developed in breathtaking decorative patterns that maintain a disciplined regularity far removed from the baroque profusion that sometimes overwhelms Benin art.

Other areas where bronze-casting techniques are used in sculpture include Iddah, near the confluence of the Niger and Benue rivers in Nigeria; one of the most celebrated examples from this region is the famous figure of an archer whose face is criss-crossed by tribal marks, and whose helmet bears an emblem embossed with a representation of the mythical bird that forever renews its life force by eating its own entrails, a recurrent figure depicted in isolation in Baoule wood sculpture.

Gold and iron sculpture

Although it is hazardous to postulate a possible direct relation between iron, bronze and gold sculpture in areas ranging from the region of Idda in Nigeria through Yorubaland and the Benin kingdom to the Ashanti of present-day Ghana and the Baoule of the Ivory Coast, there are none the less some striking similarities which occasionally create the impression that there may have been an interchange of styles in the process of transfer of techniques from one area to the other. There are, for instance, many striking similarities in the forms and stylistic patterns to be found in the production of gold ornaments among the Benin, the Ashanti and the Baoule (the latter group being an Ashanti offshoot). Metal sculpture perhaps reached its greatest heights in some of the metal funerary emblems (*assein*) of the kings of the Abomey kingdom of Dahomey, in which the attributive symbols of the deceased ruler were vigorously wrought on a metal stem. An outstanding example of Dahomean (Fon) iron sculpture is the astonishing statue of the god Goun, now in the Musée de l'Homme in Paris. In Yorubaland, the emblems of the *ogboni* secret political societies and the lamp stands designed for ritual worship also offer interesting illustrations of accomplished iron sculpture.

Form and expression in African arts

The attributive symbols inspired by allegorical sayings in Dahomey court art offer a very interesting example of the use of symbols for expressing ideas. Thus King Gezo's reign is symbolized by a calabash pierced with holes in memory of his dictum that 'if all the sons of the nation put one finger each to stop the calabash of state from leaking, the nation would be saved', while King Gbehanzin is represented by the image of a shark, in commemoration of his opposition to colonial conquests of Dahomey which led him to declare allegorically on accession to the throne that he would be 'the shark that spreads terror in the nation's coastal waters'. Such symbols form an elaborately worked pattern and represent a decorative outgrowth of the ceremonial axes utilized by court messengers to indicate royal mandate; they were also used as relief decorations on palace walls, along with other symbols commemorating significant national events, such as spectacular victories in battle over rival kingdoms, or women into special tapestries.

Architecture

African architecture has seldom given rise to massive monuments and constructions, with the possible exception of the city of Zimbabwe, a walled fortress on the east coast of Africa whose ruins attest to elaborate stone architecture. It is mostly devoted to structures of modest proportions. The reason for this is probably to be found in the imperatives of tropical climate, which led to the widespread use of clay as a building material rather than stone, with a resultant limitation of structural flourish. The typical African house is a thatch-roofed bungalow which forms part of a complex of similar habitations enclosed within a fenced compound. In spite of their basic simplicity, these habitations often achieve sculptural intensity through remarkable balance in volume and form. It is however in the decorative embellishments of buildings that the artistic genius of African peoples has most strongly asserted itself. Varying decorative patterns are sculpted or painted on walls and wooden doors, and may range from figurative designs to complex abstract patterns which reveal an exquisite balance of form, colour and shade. Indeed, it may be said that painting has traditionally

Ola Balogun

been carried out in Africa as an adjunct to architecture, rather than as an independent medium. African mural painting is both remarkably sophisticated and extremely inventive, and there is no doubt that the principles of non-figurative art as practised by twentieth-century European artists have long been in widespread application on the African continent.

The architectural legacy of the Sudanese kingdoms and cities attests to a highly successful combination of architectural and decorative achievement. Thus the famed metropoles of Sudanese civilization, such as Timbuctu, Gao and Djenne, reflect a distinct 'Sudanese' style beyond the influence of Islamic architecture, while the royal palaces of kingdoms, such as Mossi, Ashanti, Dahomey, Bamileke, Yoruba, Nupe, Kanem-Bornu, etc., reflect sophisticated and richly patterned architectural achievement.

Pottery

Paradoxically, it may be said that it is in the art of pottery that African architectural talent has reached its greatest development, in a sort of perfect blend with the innate mastery of sculptural form that is a constant in African art. Pottery is a widespread art form which combines volume design and form structure flowing out of architectural and sculptural skill, with decorative patterning reminiscent of carving and painting.

Painting

The Tassili rock paintings of the Sahara and the rock paintings of the Kalahari desert represent examples of pictural art divorced from architecture, in which painting can be considered as an isolated art. These paintings range from crude figurative drawings to extremely sophisticated stylized pictural compositions, and generally depict herdsmen and cattle, hunters, dancers, mysterious semi-human figures and wild animals. The figures are generally gracefully drawn, and contrary to stylistic practice in most other forms of African art, are depicted in motion or in moments of tension arising from a continuing state of physical activity. Usually etched in chrome, the rock paintings are generally of isolated figures or groups

Form and expression in African arts

of figures and animals in complete isolation from any landscape. They are often naturalistic in style and conceptualization, especially in relation to animal figures, but tend towards abstract stylization in representing human figures.

As we have already noted, however, painting in the African context is seldom practised as an isolated genre, and is generally found as an adjunct to architecture. Weaving and textile design for cloth manufacture also provides considerable scope for plastic creativity of the type normally associated with painting, while other domestic arts, such as skin tattooing and hair plaiting, occasion considerable decorative and plastic craftsmanship.

COMMUNICATIVE ARTS

We have seen that in discussing African art forms, it is necessary to re-examine the basic concept of art from the point of view of its finality and of its content and form. It is in this light that we find it possible to classify as art an object conceived to serve a religious or ritual role, on the basis of the treatment of form and the creative conceptualization of content. The problem is however even more complex when it comes to the realm of what is generally described as the 'performing arts'. Strictly speaking, few forms of art can be described as performing arts in the African context, in the same sense as the shadow theatre of Far East Asia, for instance, or the ballet dance theatre or operatic performance of Western European civilization, that is to say in the sense of a form of entertainment more or less openly divorced from a specific ritual or religious setting. Some instances of creative art forms which belong to this range of art are the ancient masquerade theatre of the Yoruba of Nigeria, the *Irin Ajo* masquerades, the *halo* popular theatre of the Fon of present-day Togo, a form of story mime theatre performance led by a stock character known as *hounto*, whose running commentary and mime establishes a connection between the audience and the action, and some of the performances of traditional story-tellers whose art may be described as a form of 'one-man theatre'.

Many forms of ritual ceremony and folk gatherings however include a dramatic and communicative dimension, and often incorporate dance and music, masquerade displays, and poetic chants in

Ola Balogun

one dynamic whole which derives its significance from the ritual context of the performance. In other words, as in the case of sculpture and carving conceived for ritual purposes, we are confronted with an art form whose fundamental object is to serve as a vehicle for collective manifestation of belief in sacred ritual.

For instance, the descendants of the great Songhai ruler, Sonni Ali Ber, in the present-day Niger Republic often perform a ritual dance which incorporates music, dance, and significant dramatic gestures in the course of a public gathering watched by large groups of people, yet these performances can hardly be said to be for entertainment purposes. Each Sonianke (as the descendants of Sonni Ali are known) goes through a complex dance pattern said to have been invented by the great warrior-ruler. Each warrior dances separately, holding a leafy branch in the left hand and a spear or sword in the right hand; he is followed by a praise singer and by a group of drummers. Every few steps, the warrior makes a stabbing motion towards the earth with his sword or spear in a gesture that symbolizes the age-old combat between the Sonianke and the Tierko, bad spirits held to be responsible for spreading evil among men. Each time a Sonianke makes a thrusting gesture with his weapon, a Tierko perishes. The dance performed by the Sonianke is thus fundamentally a magic act, and no ordinary dance step designed to please and amuse the onlooker. Indeed, the Sonianke dances in a state of trance, trembling in a manner that reveals the pressure of almost unbearable internal forces, carried beyond his physical limits as an individual into intense participation in his role as an embodiment of the essence of his clan. It is thus not surprising to find that at the culminating point of the dance, when the drumming has reached an intensity of frenzy, one or more of the Sonianke begins to disgorge a metal or glass-like chain from his mouth, symbolizing the unbroken chain of power transmitted by the ancestors, in a moment of supreme communion between the present and the past of the Sonianke clan, and between the material and spiritual dimensions of the clan's existence.

A phenomenon of the nature of the Sonianke ritual dance raises several questions. On the one hand, it comprises several distinct elements which, taken singly, may be considered as art forms: music, dance steps, oral poetry as reflected in the chanting of praise singers, and mime as embodied in the enactment of combat between the Sonianke and the Tierko. And yet, the finality of the whole is far from having an artistic purpose as such, in the sense generally associated with performing arts as a creative elaboration for the benefit of fee-paying spectators. We may admire the grace and rhythm of the Sonianke warrior as he dances, or the virtuosity of the drummers or the praise singers, but the fact remains that the performance cannot meaningfully be held outside the specific context and occasion for which it was conceived, and its success or failure is almost entirely dependent on the ritual function which it aims at achieving. Are we not then in the presence of art? Certainly, in so far as the form through which ritual content is expressed reflects a striving for formal perfection that incorporates elements derived from individual art forms such as dance, music, oral poetry and dramatic gesture. The Sonianke warrior does not seek to perform as an artist in the strict sense of the word, but in so far as the ritual which he enacts in the course of a collective ceremonial utilizes artistic elements as a vehicle for the manifestation of ritual content, he may be said to manipulate artistic factors to achieve his end, hence the artistic dimension in the ritual performance.

Another example may be taken from the *Edzingi* dance of the Bangombe Pygmies of the Republic of the Congo. This is a dance which is performed by hunters in the community to celebrate their success in killing any outstanding male elephant with particularly large tusks, and to placate the spirit of the dead animal through a ritual re-enactment of its death agony. In the course of the performance, a mythical animal known as *Edzingi* appears among the villagers in the form of a raphia-clad dancer. The hunters press around the *Edzingi* as he dances in acrobatic spirals to the sound of singing and clapping of hands, until he sinks to the ground in defeat and returns to the forest after lying inert for a brief period. Again, we are confronted with a phenomenon which is not strictly within the realm of art, even though it is intimately linked with artistic expression in a vehicular role. While the dance steps performed by the hunters and by the *Edzingi* may be admired in an isolated context and may even be perceived as part of a complex choreography worthy of stage performance in the best Bolshoi tradition, the fact remains that neither this choreography nor the accompanying music that forms the background to the dance, nor even the element of dramatic mime that forms the backbone of the choreography can be isolated from the ritual background that is the origin and the linking factor of the performance as a whole. We are within the realm of art in so far as formal perfection in the plastic sense is sought for each element in the performance, but the magico-ritual function of the performance belongs to an entirely different level of activity.

It is thus necessary to circumscribe carefully our definition of art in considering manifestations of the type described above, lest we fall into the error of ascribing artistic motivation where it does not belong. The artistic factor in this case is to be found in the communicative dimension, but is not in itself the end purpose of the performance, although the effectiveness of ritual is often linked to formal perfection. It would therefore perhaps be more appropriate to speak of communicative arts rather than of 'performing arts' in this context.

Ritual drama

One of the most fascinating fields of communicative arts among African peoples is to be found in performances or festival activities that emphasize dramatic action and gestures linked with ritual or religious concepts. Masquerade performances among nearly all African peoples are a typical example of this form of communicative art. In general, the masquerade, as we have already seen, is a physical embodiment of a non-materialized entity (divinity, spirit or ancestor), whose presence is communicated to spectators of the masquerade festival through the appearance, actions and dances of a costumed masquerade player. In these displays, the dimension of ritual drama dominates, for the masquerade or masquerades, are performers in a collective dramatic representation which evokes physical interaction between men and gods. In the final analysis, the mask and the costume of the masquerade are in a sense theatre props which enable the masquerade player to act out the role of the divine being or spirit whose presence the display purports to communicate. The mask and the costume are thus adjuncts in the ritual drama of the appearance among men of the divine being whose role the masquerade player performs, in the same way as the crown and royal robes donned by the Shakespearian actor who plays King Lear are adjuncts in a dramatic performance, the purpose being in each case to enable the actor or performer to assume the personality of the character in the play, or the divinity in the masquerade performance. The similarity also extends to the fact that the actor must utter words deemed to be spoken by the play character, and manifest behavorial traits that reflect the personality and the actions of the play character, while the masquerade player must also walk, behave and dance in a manner deemed to be characteristic of the spirit or god whom he represents, as well as make utterances or sounds or sing words that are deemed to be spoken by the divine being or deceased ancestor. Thus a fiery spirit charges aggressively at bystanders, a female spirit dances graceful steps typifying feminity, and an animal spirit generally reproduced the behaviour traits of the particular animal it represents through symbolically mimed gestures. In both cases also, a temporary suspension of disbelief is demanded of the spectator, whose participative acceptance of the reality of the figures who people the drama stage or appear in the masquerade display is often necessary if the play or masquerade action is to have its full impact. The resemblance however ends on the level of the actor's psychological motivation and inner participatory action, for the actor is only conscious that he is acting, while the masquerade player, though conscious to some extent that he has to act out a role in a clearly defined manner, is primarily motivated by the magico-psychic awareness of induced identity with the divinity or spirit whose role he plays. He becomes the divinity, whose personality temporarily takes over his own personality, rather than seeks to act out the role of a being conceived of as being external to himself. This is a vital factor indeed, and explains why most masquerade displays cannot simply take place in any kind of context, without being integrated into an appropriate ritual in which sacrifices, ritual invocations, etc., play an important part. In the end, the masquerade player merely 'lends' his body to the spirit that inhabits the masquerade, and the ritual observances that precede the performance are an indispensable means of effecting this transfer. This in fact means that without the magico-ritual dimension, the masquerade performance loses its true significance and is shorn of the

Ola Balogun

source of part of its dramatic effectiveness. The masquerade performance may therefore best be described as a multi-facetted whole which includes music, dance, ritual drama, and magico-ritual symbols (the mask for instance is both a theatre-type prop and an object imbued with magic power) which together are of artistic significance as an adjunct or a vehicle for a religious rite.

There may however be variations in the degree of religious significance of the masquerade performance, and some masquerade displays are known to have evolved considerably from an originally sacred function to a stage where the dramatic and entertaining dimensions of the display tend to dominate religious content. This is the case of some of the *Ekine* plays of the Kalabari of the Niger delta area of Nigeria, of which an interesting example is the *Ikaki* or tortoise masquerade. The origin of this play has its roots in a magico-religious aspect of Kalabari social life, as is clearly demonstrated by the fact that the Kalabari believe that the dance was first performed by a mysterious tortoise-like spirit, a kind of embodiment of tortoise-essence on a divine level. After the mythical *Ikaki* disappeared from human view, the villagers who had watched its dancing decided to imitate its dance, which they were able to do after appropriate religious rites designed to protect the dancers and invoke the participation of the mythical tortoise divinity in their performance. While not being entirely divorced from this early religious association (sacrifices still have to be performed, and the magic element is still present to some extent), the *Ikaki* masquerade has gradually become primarily an occasion for social entertainment and dancing displays. The display itself begins with the appearance of *Ikaki* in colourful masquerade attire, complete with hump-back shell and a carved tortoise mask worn on top of the head, accompanied by his two children *Nimite Poku* (know all) and *Nimiaa Poku* (know nothing). The trio clown their way to the beach, watched by joyous townsfolk who exchange taunts and warnings with the masquerades, accompanied by drumming and dancing. There, they board a canoe, which they attempt to row out to sea, and tortoise sits confidently in the prow, while 'know all' paddles forward and the dullard 'know nothing' takes to bailing water into the canoe instead of doing the reverse, and the voyage nearly ends in disaster before the canoe pulls back to the shore. This highly comic episode is followed by displays of dancing and acrobatics by the inimitable trio, who are occasionally joined in dancing and singing by the townsfolk.

The *Ikaki* masquerade may be said to be an example of a masquerade display in which the dramatic and entertaining aspects tend to be of dominant importance, as in the *Irin ajo* Yoruba masquerade. This is clearly distinct as a form of display designed to entertain onlookers from the more widespread *Egungun* masquerade display in which the magical evocation of ancestral or spirit entitles is the determining factor, although a certain degree of this magical atmosphere is not absent from the *Irin Ajo* masquerade. The vital difference however is that the *Egungun* display has a religious object, while the *Irin Ajo* is a travelling theatre (as its name indicates) conceived for entertainment purposes.

In the same way that the ritual drama associated with masquerade performances is a dominant factor, some of the possession rites that are part of certain religious ceremonies and activities among various African peoples have a strong element of dramatic display. There are two distinct categories of such rites, although both operate through the same mechanisms: there are rites utilized for the purpose of healing mentally disturbed or physically ill individuals through temporary assumption of the personality of a divine entity or spirit associated with the particular illness, and rites that serve as part of the worship of a divine entity or spirit through a similar process involving temporary assumption of its personality by a devotee or priest. Typical examples of the former are the *n'deup* possession cult of the Wolof people of Senegal and the *bori* possession cult of the Hausa and Fulani peoples of the northern Cameroons, Chad, Nigeria and Niger Republic. In Hausaland for instance, the *Bori* cult was originally derived from the worship of indigenous divinities of the pre-Islamic period, but has grown to absorb both Moslem spirits and all other assimilable new influences, including spirits derived from colonial sources. The Muslim spirits are known as *Yan Riga* (from the flowing muslim robes), headed by Dan Alhaji, while the bush spirits are know as *Yan Dowa* (literally Children of the Bush), while specifically indigenous pre-Islamic spirits are known as *Babbaku*, headed by *Mai-Ja-Ciki*. Warrior spirits are known as *Yan Garki*, headed by

Garki Baba, and other categories include spirits associated with specific illnesses such as smallpox (*Yayanzanzanna*). The spirits are believed to be living within organized communities in the same manner as human beings, and each individual spirit is associated with a specific form of social behaviour, psychic state, or physical illness. During the *bori* dance, which is mainly performed by women, *bori* performers dance to the music of drummers and fiddlers, and assume the personality of the specific spirit with which their own individuality has close correlation. The possessed person is said to serve as a mount for the spirit by which she is possessed, and behaves in a manner that reflects the known attributes and personality traits of the spirit during the dance performed in a state of trance. The *bori* dance, like the *n'deup* dance, permits diagnosis and treatment of various psychic disorders by reference to the spirit which possesses the sick individual. If she is possessed by one spirit rather than the other, she is known to be suffering from an illness or psychic disorder associated with that spirit, and efforts are made to relieve the illness by provoking a catharsis through deliberate simulation of the identified disorder in the course of possession trances. The *bori* dance also serves the more general purpose of regulating certain social activities and relationships and also provides a compensatory factor for social adjustment, where maladjustment is a functional outgrowth of the total socio-cultural setting. The *bori* dancer becomes an embodiment of the spirit by which she is deemed to have been mounted during the duration of the trance-like state provoked by possession. Again, we are confronted with the utilization of elements belonging to the sphere of artistic endeavour (i.e. music dance, dramatic performance, etc.) within the context of a socio-cultural rite which does not have artistic achievement as its finality, but in which plastic perfection and entertainment are nonetheless achieved. The spectator is undoubtedly entertained, and derives pleasure from watching the performance, but the artistic element here lies in the function of the performance as a vehicle for a non-artistic purpose.

Another illustration is to be found in a different category of possession rite, in which a devotee or priest is possessed by a divinity or spirit entity as part of a ritual of worship. A striking example of this phenomenon appears in the Yoruba cult of Shango, the thunder divinity. During the annual festival in honour of Shango at Ede—one of the Yoruba towns in which the Shango cult is still actively practised—part of the festival features devotees who perform displays of magic prowess and dancing while they are deemed to be 'mounted' by Shango. These displays may be described as mi-ritual theatre, mi-popular entertainment, and are by far the most spectacular aspect of the festival. The devotee who becomes possessed by Shango comports himself as an archetypal manifestation of the god, and is in fact deemed to be the living avatar of Shango. The 'mount' may be said to be 'acting' the role of Shango, not as the stage actor who consciously acts a role, but rather in the sense of assuming the personality of Shango. We are in fact witnessing a religious ceremony, and the performances of the god's 'mount' are a symbol of society's communication with Shango.

'TRADITIONAL' ART AND MODERN ART

In this brief survey of African art forms, we have dwelt mostly on the more traditional patterns of creative arts among African peoples, since modern art forms would more naturally find their place in the chapter on contemporary African culture. This does not however mean that we perceive an irrevocable divorce between past and present African art, even though some changes have been provoked by the influence of Western European culture as a result of the colonial experience.

In reality, the apparent dichotomy between the so-called traditional artist and the Western-oriented 'modern' African artist lies in the fact that in most cases, the latter has turned his back on his own artistic heritage in favour of an alien one. This induced imitation of Western European art is not a case of evolution from the 'primitive' to the 'modern', as some would have us believe, but part of the cultural conflict created by the colonial occupation of the African continent by Western European powers. The so-called 'modern' African artist is not, in most cases, in any sense modern as opposed to his predecessors, but simply Western-oriented. Ironically enough, his orientation is often towards art forms that have long ceased to be considered modern in the western world. If he is a musician, he insists on composing symphonies and operas at a

Ola Balogun

time when his counterparts in the West have long given up such forms, because he has been led to believe that symphonic music is more 'civilized' than his own musical heritage. If a painter, he derives inordinate pride from having learnt to paint in perspective, when his counterparts in the West have come to consider such accomplishments as belonging to an irretrievable past, and are engaged in practising a 'modern' art largely influenced by 'traditional' African sculpture!

There are however many genuinely creative contemporary African artists, whose work reflects continuity with past African art forms, even though they live in a physical and environmental setting which is very different from that of their predecessors. There are also many interesting evolutionary outgrowths from traditional art forms, as in the appearance of musical styles influenced by African-derived musical traditions from the Caribbean and the Americas, and in the achievements of professional ballet groups like the National Guinean Ballet, who have succeded in incorporating various elements of communicative arts, such as ritual and folk dances and music, into coherent and well-choreographed dance displays. A new body of literature and new forms of performing arts also reflect the basic African capacity to absorb new influences judiciously within the framework of indigenous creative artistry.

There is no doubt, then, that far from being 'dead', African art forms have continued to evolve satisfactorily, both within the framework of traditional socio-cultural structures and on the level of contemporary art forms resulting directly or indirectly from contact with the Western world. Provided that adequate efforts are made to preserve the African cultural heritage in an authentic cadre and to promote the growth of contemporary art forms in a direction which is faithful to the spirit and internal dynamism of the cultural heritage of African peoples, there is every reason to believe that African art will rapidly win long-overdue recognition as one of the world's major families of artistic creativity.

Form and expression in African arts

BIBLIOGRAPHY

BEBEY, Francis. *Musique de l'Afrique*. Paris, Horizons de France, 1969.

FAGG, William; PLASS, Margaret. *African Sculpture*. London, Studio Vista, 1964.

HORTON, Robin. *Kalatari Sculpture*. Lagos, Federal Department of Antiquities.

HUET, Michel, *et al*. *Afrique Africaine*. Lausanne, La Guilde du Livre.

LEUZINGER, E. *Afrique. Art des Peuples Noirs*. Paris, Albin Michel, 1962.

LHOTE, Henry. *A la Découverte des Fresques du Tassili*. Paris, Arthaud, 1973.

MEAUZE, Pierre. *African Art*. Cleveland and New York, World Publishing Company, 1968.

NDONG NDOUTOUME, Teire. *Le Mvett*. Paris, Présence Africaine, 1975.

NIANE, D. T. *Soundjata ou l'Époque Mandigue*. Paris, Présence Africaine, 1960.

PRÉSENCE AFRICAINE. *Colloque sur l'Art Nègre*. Paris, Présence Africaine, 1967. (Rapport du Premier Festival Mondial des Arts Nègres.)

UNDERWOOD, Leon. *Bronzes of West Africa*. London, Alec Tiranti, 1968.

——. *Masks of West Africa*. London, Alec Tiranti, 1964.

Traditional African views and apperceptions

Honorat Aguessy

> *One does not know everything. All that one knows is a part of everything.* Fulani proverb.

When an author undertakes a study of culture in Europe, his first reflex is to turn to other writers for his references. The European cultural field is defined by the totality of the writings by all previous authors; and it is the knowledge and mastery of this field which reveals the cultivated man.

But with Africa—Africa as a whole—the case is far different. There the primary fact about culture is not the written word but oral expression. This inevitably entails special consequences, not only as to the sources of cultural values, but also as to the status and the practical function of the various conditions and means of transmitting its particular world view.

What, then, is specifically African about the various African views of the universe, life and society? It would be surprising if non-African societies had never had at least comparable ideas on these matters.

Is one justified in speaking, from the outset, about external influences (a hypothesis which has always obsessed certain ethno-centric European writers)? It would be too easy, each time that different human societies exhibit similarities of one kind or another, to resort to the theory imposed by the current balance of power in the world and exclaim, 'No, these works of art could never have been conceived by Africans in the sixth century B.C.! They are surely the result of European contacts and influences.' Such is the unfailing reaction of many Europeans on being introduced, for instance, to Noko objects, or more precisely to Ife figurines.

The only intellectual attitude which promotes understanding and heuristics consists—for the man of culture at least—in ridding the mind of the prejudices produced by the will to dominate, which finds expression mainly in politics.

Claude Lévi-Strauss's observation about the logical aptitudes of different societies is to the point here:

In the same way we may be able to show that the same logical processes operate in myth as in science, and that man has always been thinking equally well: the improvement lies, not in an alleged progress of man's mind, but in the discovery of new areas to which it may apply its unchanged and unchanging powers.[1]

From this point of view, the distinctiveness of the African outlook on the universe and society does not consist in superior qualities of intellect—or, for that matter, in inferior qualities. It is to be found in the cultural environment (including ecology) as it is dialectically transformed.

I say 'dialectically transformed' because there is an exchange between the environment and the intellect, a transformation of the environment by the products of the intellect, a readaptation of the intellect to the transformed environment (including changes owing to contacts with other societies).

Such being the case, different variables have to be considered before defining the *proprium africanum*. What are these variables?

First, there are the ecological and geographical conditions (climate, seasons, floods, precipitation): the differences between the savannah and the rain-forest, the hydrographic variations which may explain the modalities of population distribution and communication, and the different emphases in African thought. For example, one can speak of the way of thinking of the farmers in the savannah, or the hunters in the steppe country, or the pastoralists (the Masai, the Nuer, the Shilluk), or the forest dwellers, or the civilizations of the great empires (the Mossi, the Ashanti, the Yoruba, the Bamoun, the Bini, etc.).

1. Claude Lévi-Strauss, *Structural Anthropology*, p. 230. Translated from the French by Claire Jacobson and Brooke Grundfest Schoepf. London, Allen Lane The Penguin Press, 1968.

Secondly, one has to take into account the 'size' and 'bulk' of the societies being studied—whether they are small closed societies, or larger societies open to the outside. The contrast between the isolation of the small groups and the large groups' multiplicity of contacts ('the sources of numerous borrowings and differentiations') may result in a different emphasis being laid on this or that feature of their view and perception of the world.

Thirdly, one must consider the kind of mentality produced by the particular history of a given African society. Thus the fairly advanced culture of the Nok, based on working iron and tin, carving statuettes, manufacturing a wide range of pottery, and a technically sophisticated agriculture, resulted in a different mentality from that of the Hottentot or Pygmy cultures.

In short, any definition of African distinctiveness must take into account the different cultural inflections produced by the following three types of variable: the physical, the socio-economic and the historical.

Are these requirements respected by the numerous authors who attempt to define the distinctiveness of the African conception of the universe, life and society?

I do not intend to give a detailed evaluation here of the findings of the various studies carried out along these lines, such as the work of Marcel Griaule, Father Tempels, Melville Herskovits, Lucien Lévy-Bruhl, Bascom and others. Though Lévy-Bruhl is known chiefly for his ideologically inspired book, *La Mentalité Primitive*, and Father Tempels has come to the notice of Europeans thanks to his *Philosophie Bantoue*, Herskovits and Griaule have devoted dozens of publications (no less than eighty-odd titles—articles and books—by Griaule alone!) to the problems with which we are dealing here. A complete appraisal of these works would be tedious and does not come within the scope of the present study.

Nevertheless, a quick survey of the different European writings on the question shows that they generally emphasize three principles in defining Africa's conception of the world: 'Life, Force and Unity are the three major principles' of the traditional world views and apperceptions. In this connection, some European thinkers have asked, 'How can one account philosophically for the fact that systems of thought which grant so large a place to the living, propulsive,

dynamic aspect of being, have not resulted in more advanced technological progress? Why did Africa not evolve scientifically prior to
colonization?' They wonder whether the lack of orientation leading
to the evolution of a more industrial form of production might not
be explained, in part at least, by too great an attachment to Mother
Earth, thus preventing natural resources—except when strictly
necessary—from being removed, 'so as not to wear her out and
render her weak-blooded and feeble.'[1]

Louis-Vincent Thomas shows how the following three key
ideas may account for the character of African thought, resulting in
a sort of impressionistic perception of the world: (a) a sort of
contamination at the conceptual level (for example, of the material
by the spiritual view, and vice versa); (b) a reluctance to question
nature and the origins of beings and things; and (c) a notorious
inability to shift from ideology to logical action.

In most of the works which attempt to probe the African
cultural field, the extraordinary complexity of Africa's unitary view
of the world is stressed. Different levels of existence and different
beings are unified by the 'life force'. The different beings are the
supreme being, the various supernatural beings (gods and spirits),
the souls of the dead (ancestors), living men, the vegetable, mineral
and animal realm, the realm of magic. One could represent the world,
as seen from this point of view, by a triangle, with the supreme being
at its apex and surrounding it, the lesser magical powers at its base,
the ancestors and supernatural beings at its two other sides, and
lastly man inside it, symbolized by a small circle surrounded evenly
by the material realm. That gives one a rough idea of the African
world view, in which the universe (with its different realms), life and
society are inextricably interconnected and perceived as a symbiotic
unit. The life force is not a separate concept: the spontaneity and
endless continuity of its flow make this unit a dynamic system.

Can one compare this life force with the *vis viva* of Leibnitz,
about which we are told that it is something

different from the magnitude of the figure and the movement; and from
this it can be inferred that all that is conceived in the body does not

1. Marie de Paul Neiers, *La Philosophie de Quelques Tribus de la Région de Jos
Nigeria—Théologie, Cosmologie, Anthropologie* (thesis presented in 1974).

Traditional African views and apperceptions

consist solely in its reach and in its modifications, as modern thinkers believe, so that we are therefore obliged to reintroduce certain beings or forms which they had banished (*Discours de Métaphysique*)?

Can one compare it with Bergson's *élan vital*, which reveals itself in the spatial deployment of emerging species, or as a simple tendency underlying the complex ramifications of the genealogy of beings? Or should one understand this life force rather as the dynamic expression of the fruitful contradictions embedded in all beings? Whatever the case, thinkers who tackle this subject rely on an impressive number of metaphors.

Take Janheinz Jahn[1], who writes:

Ntu is the term which designates the basic concept of forces, the primordial realm of energy; it is not itself an object of veneration. Nor is the mythical representative of this realm of energy—whether he is called 'God', Nya-Murunga, the 'Great Begetter' Olorum, Amma, Vidye, Immana, the Lord, or anything else—any more capable of making a personal contact with man. . . . Ntu is the universal force as such, purely and simply. . . . Ntu is the force being and becoming coincide in. The contradictions which vexed André Breton do not occur in Ntu. . . . Ntu consists of things themselves; it is not an added determination.

Another author borrows from linguistics in order to clarify this notion of life force:

This philosophy . . . might be compared to a sentence stating an original message: it is composed of various elements (verb, subject, object, adjectives, adverb, etc.) each of which is indispensable to the total meaning, but which, once it is isolated in logical analysis, offers nothing more than a small, lifeless fraction of that meaning, and does not reveal that which is signified. But the expression 'life force' is the verb, lacking which the contents would be dead and meaningless. It is not surprising then that, in order to begin translating the message, one must first locate the verb.

Jahn too stresses the importance of the verb. While reminding us of various aspects of the inextricable interrelationship between life, the universe and society (Muntu is 'an essence which is power and

1. Janheinz Jahn, *Muntu, l'Homme Africain et la Culture Néo-Africaine*, p. 127. Paris, Le Seuil, 1961. Translated by Brian de Martinou.

to which the mastery of the Nommo belongs', 'the human soul, during a man's life, does not even have a separate name in our philosophy' (Kagame), 'everything is concentrated on the precious aliveness of living men who perpetuate life transmitted by the ancestors'), Jahn notes that 'the active impulse which sets all these forces in motion is the *Nommo*, the verb'[1] which can be represented by the spoken word, by water or by sperm.

Louis-Vincent Thomas likewise draws attention to the role of the verb:

The conception of an arbitrary, obscure and irrational world seems altogether foreign to traditional Africa. Before anything, the black man invests the universe as a whole, as well as its constituent parts and the phenomena which occur within it, with meaning. By humanizing nature—or rather by making it hominine—as a system of intentions and signs, he asserts his own power. And he has such faith in the power of his verb that he will not undertake any action (hollowing out a pirogue, preparing poison, sowing a field) without first uttering the ritual words without which no action could be successfully completed.[2]

Much has been said and written on this subject. So far I have mainly quoted French-speaking authors. But just as many passages along the same lines could be taken from the English-speaking writers, like Bascom, Evans-Pritchard, Fortes, Middleton, Radcliff-Brown, Tait, etc.

The question that arises is to what extent are we confronted with statements which, while not being entirely false, are nevertheless neither accurate nor true at all levels? To what extent are we dealing with theories which are 'sometimes brilliant, but sterile and removed from reality'? How is one to explain the fact that each one of these authors recognizes his favourite philosophical system in the African world view, with the result that one scholar speaks of Platonism, another of Aristotelianism, another of Augustinian thought, another of Thomistic thought, yet another of Nietzsche or Bergson, etc.? Is there indeed something arbitrary about all these approaches; and if so, what does it stem from?

1. Jahn, op. cit., p. 112, 119, 121.
2. L.-V. Thomas, *Les Religions de l'Afrique Noire*, p. 14, Paris, Fayard, Denoël, 1969.

Here is what one European has to say about this matter:

From the vantage point of his large or small experience of a black country, no matter who from no matter where believes himself qualified and almost duty bound to pass a crisp, definitive—and, incidentally, unoriginal—judgement on the black man. This kind of 'expert' will always skim the surface of Africa without ever getting beneath it; other men, on the contrary—and I am speaking of Europeans—are able to view Africa as a new world with more to be discovered each passing day.[1]

Snap judgements about African societies tend to produce their own difficulties. One of the most obvious is the controversy among Europeans about whether one can speak of philosophy proper in Africa. Consider for instance the following divergency of opinions between Marcel Griaule, Louis-Vincent Thomas and Janheinz Jahn (though the three men have never debated the point directly).

In his many articles ('Art et Symbole en Afrique Noire', 'La Civilization Dogon', 'L'Image du Monde au Soudan', 'Les Religions Noires', etc.) and especially in his books, *Dieu d'Eau* (conversations with Ogotemmêli) and *Le Renard Pâle*, Marcel Griaule defends the notion that philosophy exists in Africa. This is proved beyond question, he believes, by his Dogon informer, Ogotemmêli, whose ideas on the universe, life, society and the genesis of the world astounded Griaule.

L. V. Thoma's views on the question are expressed in somewhat veiled terms:

The originality of modern ethnology lies in its having given prominence to the African philosophies, which, we are told, are comparable and even superior to Greek metaphysics [M. Griaule] or to Cartesian thought [R. P. Tempels]. While stressing the fact that these judgements reveal a relative ignorance [obvious in Tempels' case] of the European philosophers, one cannot but regard such claims as excessive. Admittedly, there is a layman's sense of the word philosophy, according to which any man who reflects a little, strives to arrive at a few general ideas about the world, and connects his moral conduct to a few elements of cosmogeny, may be called a philosopher. In this sense, there is a Diola philosophy

1. Neiers, op. cit., p. 303.

Honorat Aguessy

because there is a Diola *modus vivendi*. The dynamic conception of the universe, the hierarchy of forces, the law of anticipation . . . undoubtedly all have power and depth. But a genuine philosophy involves the notion of system, and presupposes both synthesis and abstraction, two features of thought which do not seem widespread in Black Africa. . . . Furthermore a genuine philosophy calls for logical justification, for thought to take a step back in order to evaluate itself, but the critical spirit is not an inherent quality of the African soul, which is more sensual than reflective, more mystical than epistemological. . . . Negro-African ethnological traditions and conceptions constitute a body which can only seldom be described as philosophy in the strict sense of ontological investigation expressed within a painstakingly developed system.[1]

The debate does not stop there. Janheinz Jahn, who uses the term 'traditional philosophy' in chapter four of his book, *Ntu*, states that philosophy is the 'corner-stone of African culture'. 'Perhaps', he says, 'it will be objected that philosophical thought presupposes a deliberate rationalization of things, and that no such example is to be found in Africa's past, which offers only myths.' But this objection has already been refuted, he believes: as soon as there is conscious thought, the image of the world which was formerly a matter of belief, intuition and daily experience, is transformed into philosophy. Friedell writes:

Each thing has its philosophy, [or rather], each thing is philosophy. Man's task is to seek out the idea concealed within each fact, and to pursue within each fact the idea of which it is but a simple form.

Janheinz Jahn concludes:[2]

Since we are dealing with an African philosophy, and not a variety of European thought, it is obviously hazardous to try and fit that thought into the mould of European vocabulary.

Though this debate is hotly argued by foreign experts, it does not seem to have had any effect on the African cultures. It is not because a given thinker has declared that Africa possesses philosophies

1. L. V. Thomas, *Essai d'Analyse Fonctionnelle sur une Population de Basse-Casamance*, p. 821, Dakar, IFAN.
2. Jahn, op. cit., p. 25.

comparable or even superior to those known in Europe or elsewhere that the status of the traditional African cultures will be raised. Nor because a thinker, however eminent, may have decreed that no philosophy exists in Africa, but only views and perceptions of the world, disconnected ideas without synthesis or abstract thought, will the values generated and renewed by the African creative spirit disappear *ipso facto* (and as if by miracle).

If it were irrefutably demonstrated that a high level of culture depended on the mere fact of possessing a philosophy of sterile abstraction and runaway logic, I would be willing to delve deeper into the above question in order to give a more detailed account of the African world view. But if philosophy is understood as a permanent nay-saying, and if, on the psycho-analytical level, it is seen as belonging not only to the order of symbolic expression (taking advantage, in much the same way that a shaman does, of the effectiveness of symbols) but also to the delirium in which the 'I' which thinks and arrives at synthesis and abstraction comforts itself with the illusion that it is free, when in reality it is imprisoned in the texture of the cultural order which shapes it—then it would not be worth taking the trouble to refute this or that particular opinion.

My purpose instead is to offer a few explanations of the traditional African world view. These remarks are meant to rid the reader's mind (and first the writer's) of a number of prejudices which would otherwise distort the analysis.

In addition to arguing about the paucity of synthesis and abstraction in African thought, and to further belittle the cultural values produced by the creative spirit in Africa, some Europeans cite the 'Greek miracle' and express surprise at the lack of names of great African philosophers. Hypnotized by such observations, a number of Africans go so far as to make a radical distinction between philosophy, the polished gem of the 'Greek miracle', and myth, the rough ore of the sensual African soul. Thus Adebayo Adesanya:

Listening to an Ifa teacher, one is struck by the complete absence of any reference to myth in what he says. With him one enters the realm of pure thought where the pure being is contemplated within the category

Honorat Aguessy

of immutable spatio-temporal permanence. Myths are a way of solving the problem of the transmission and popular teaching of this philosophy, a way of making conclusions developed in an ivory tower intelligible in the market place.[1]

Adebayo Adesanya is a Yoruba well acquainted with Yoruba culture, but one gets the distinct impression that he tends to reason like certain Hellenists, especially Platonists,[2] who make the same distinction. Indeed these experts view the presence and even the abundance of mythological material in Plato's dialogues as stemming purely from pedagogical considerations. Thus the myths of Er the Armenian, of Poros and Penia, of Chronos, of the Cave, would seem to be of no significance in themselves, their purpose being merely to convey ideas which intellectual intuition and synoptic understanding make it possible to contemplate.

But without the myths he recounts I do not see how Plato, an eminent representative of the 'Greek miracle', could have attained the sufficient reason (*logos ikanos*) of the questions he examined. After all myth often provided him with a synthesis of the major problems he tackled. Let us come out of our hypnotic trance and calmly consider the ideology underlying such statements.

Even if one were to agree about the achievements which the Greeks may be credited with (the organization of space, the organization of political life, the transformation of social life, the development of sea trade, the development of an economy based on money, as J.-P. Vernant has shown),[3] one cannot but observe that the insistence on this Greek miracle is motivated by an extraordinary ideology. It is not a matter of an objective, neutral approach; instead a single point of emergence in space and time, and a single orientation invested with an absolute value, are assigned to the history of thought. It would be fairer to say, as Claude Lévi-Strauss does, that the emergence of philosophy in Greece consisted above all

1. Adebayo Adesanya, 'Yoruba Metaphysical Thinking', *Odu 5*, p. 41, Ibadan, 1958.
2. cf. Couturat who considers 'as alien to Plato's philosophy any passage of a mythological character' (in *De Platonicis Mythis*, Paris, 1896). Also V. Goldschmidt, for whom the Platonic myths only serve as vehicles for the supreme method, dialectics.
3. J.-P. Vernant, *Mythe et Pensée Chez les Grecs*, Paris, Maspero, 1965.

in myth being reflected upon myth in the characteristically circular movement of mythological imagination—this being true even when economic causes are taken into account.

The 'Greek miracle' prejudice which has obsessed many Western philosophers, especially Hegel, Heidegger and Husserl, must not be allowed to slant the analysis of the different cultures being considered.

Now what about the attitude of those who ask for names of great African philosophers, meaning thinkers who have brought light to metaphysical problems under the banner of their own names instead of by submerging their identity in the collective anonymity of a tradition? To be able to put one's name to a text which has been conceived, thought out and written by oneself is an admirable thing; to realize when signing a text (or not) that one is not precisely and entirely its only author is even better. No doubt thinkers are the writers of their own works, but are they really the only authors of those works? What is the relationship between the work signed by the 'thinker' and the anonymous work labelled traditional? It seems to me that the way this aspect of the problem of the status of 'traditional' cultures is approached contains ambiguities and betrays a lack of real knowledge about Africa.

In my attempt to construct an appropriate methodology for dealing with the African cultural field, I shall endeavour to define the points which seem important to me in this connection. Let us begin with the false problem of the role of the 'I' in the written work.

No value, in any form of cultural expression, whether written or oral, ever reaches the audience without first transiting, however briefly, through the individual. But the individual is not the antithesis of the community, the group. For example, where would the individual be in society without language, without a grammar and a vocabulary bequeathed to him by the community? Each individual is characterized by a personal style—a partial and always inadequate attempt to present a work that is always unfinished—but this is true only to the extent that the individual acts in a context where tradition determines the order of symbolic references which give meaning to everything that he undertakes and completes. For that matter, tradition, contrary to one's static idea of it, is in no way the mere repetition of identical sequences; by no means does it reflect a petrified state of culture which is transmitted without change from one generation to the next. Activity and change are inherent in the concept of tradition.

The individual and the group are therefore linked to each other by a thousand indissoluble ties. Such is the case, anyway, with the relationship between society and the individual as it is experienced in Africa. Society has no 'essence'—not in the sense of possessing an unchanging and timeless nature. African societies evolve within a dynamic framework; the migration of its groups constituting both a significant metaphor and a significant metonymy of this fact. Even in the midst of population movements or changes, which are synonymous with dialectical enrichment, the individual never ceases to be welded to the community.

Surprisingly this truth glimpsed superficially has led some observers to conclude dogmatically that the 'self' does not exist in Africa, that the individual is subordinated to the community. But that is only an unwarranted extrapolation verging on paralogism. Is not the case, actually, that the 'self' plays such a preponderant role in Western culture that the above observers feel the need to contrast it with a supposed absence of 'self' in Africa? Let us see what Western thinkers themselves have to say about this point.

Here, for example, is a reflection by Claude Lévi-Strauss in his book, *L'Homme Nu*:

The self's consistency, a major concern of all Western philosophy, does not stand up to being applied continuously to the same object, absorbing it entirely and imbuing it with a strongly felt sense of its own lack of reality. For the small degree of reality to which it still dares lay claim is that of a singularity, as the term is understood by astronomers: a point in space and a point in time, each being relative to the other, where events have occurred, are occurring or will occur. The density of these events, itself relative compared to other no less real but more scattered events, can be approximately circumscribed, provided that the sum of past, present and probable events does not exist as a substratum but only insofar as things occur, and despite the fact that these things, which intersect there, emerge from innumerable points elsewhere and more often than not from no one knows where.[1]

1. Claude Lévi-Strauss, *Mythologiques*, IV: *L'Homme Nu*, p. 559, Paris, Plon, 1971.

Traditional African views and apperceptions

For those who call for names of African philosophers on a par with Plato, Aristotle, Descartes, Kant, Hegel, etc., and who deny the authenticity of any culture that does not boast of outstanding individual works, it is worth recalling another thought by the same author: 'Individual works are all potential myths, but it is only their adoption by the community which, if it occurs, actualizes their "mythicality".'[1] On the other hand, there has never been a myth which did not begin with an individual imagining and narrating it, as Lévi-Strauss says clearly in the following passage:

Why . . . is one so reluctant to mention an individual creator when speaking about myths—i.e. narratives which could not have emerged without being conceived and told for the first time by an individual at some moment, even if that moment is (as is usually the case) unknowable? For it is only individuals who can be said to *tell*; and any myth must, in final resort, have originated in some individual creation.[2]

In short,

while replacing the self with, on the one hand, an anonymous *other*, and, on the other hand, an individualized desire (without which nothing would be designated), there is no hiding the fact that it suffices to join the two together and to reverse the relationship to recognize, upside down as it were, that very self whose abolition had earlier been so noisily proclaimed. If there is any moment when the self can re-emerge, it is only once it has finished the work from which it had been excluded from start to finish (for, contrary to what one might believe, the self was less the author than was the work itself, which, as it was being written, gradually became the author directing the writer, who experienced life through it, and through it alone).[3]

This kind of prejudice, which leads people to deny the philosophical aspect of African cultures and to belittle their view of the world—which is judged a source of unreal and incoherent ideas—needed to be pointed out before specifying, in a more circumspect manner, what is meant by the expression 'traditional views and

1. ibid., p. 560.
2. ibid., p. 559–60.
3. ibid., p. 563.

conceptions of the universe, life and society'. The paralogisms detected in the various pronouncements on this subject indicate the general direction to follow if the present study is to be at all relevant.

It is not my role here to state in turn that the traditional African views and conceptions of the universe consist of this or that, or that the traditional African views and apperceptions of life are of this or that order. That would simply amount to adding further assertions to the mass of all those that are already familiar to most readers. On the other hand, it seems useful here to dwell on the field of African cultural values and on the conditions under which they are produced.

First, it should be remembered that one of the characteristic features of traditional African cultures—in some respects their primary feature—is their 'orality'. In a predominantly 'scriptural' culture, the sources of values are the 'authors' and their works (which results in the cultural reflex found in some thinkers of denying the existence of thought wherever written works are not the rule). Today it is generally acknowledged that valuable cultural works can and do arise in the context of 'orality'.

Does this mean that writing has never existed in Africa? Only inadequate information about the field of African culture could lead someone to assert that Africa has produced no systems of writing, whether pictographic (symbols for ideas or words) or phonetic (syllabic or alphabetic writing). Every human society, as is now widely recognized, has some specific means of recording which permits it, to a certain extent, to appropriate time. But beyond this general statement, one must point out that, despite the existence of a system of writing among the Bamoun (Cameroon), and despite the existence of the Vai (Sierra Leone), Nsidibi (Calabar, western Nigeria), Basa and Mende scripts (Sierra Leone and Liberia), none of these societies has used writing in the same way that the Chinese and Western civilizations have. Should it be objected that the former scriptural systems are recent, dating no earlier than the nineteenth or, at best, the eighteenth centuries, one might observe that the Egyptian system, along with the Sumerian and the Chinese systems, is one of the three oldest and most important 'word-based' modes of writing. Nevertheless, in Africa, cultural values have by and large been transmitted and perpetuated orally.

Therefore when I speak of 'orality' as being characteristic of the field of African culture, I mean that it is preponderant, not exclusive. I use the term to indicate that the oral transmission of knowledge and cultural values is generally preferred, but this need not exclude a specific mode of recording and stabilizing messages.

The objection which usually springs to mind at this point is that no scientific or literary work has been written down in African culture. This is false, of course, as a closer look at the cultural dynamics of the African continent makes plain.

I will not dwell on the extraordinary cultural creations of the schools of ancient Egypt, that university crossroads which attracted men of learning from all over the world and has left a lasting mark on the history of ideas and institutions. Ever since Herodotus of Halicarnassus, in the fifth century B.C., published his observations, shedding light on the cultural ambience of that part of Africa (the 'gift of the river', as it was called), numerous scholars and learned writers have enlarged on that same topic. I need only remind the reader that Egypt's cultural heritage is an integral part of the cultural heritage of Africa. As Volney writes:

It was there that most of the beliefs which we are governed by came into being; it was there that the religious ideas which have exercised such a powerful influence on our political and individual ethics, on our laws and our whole state of society, emerged. Therefore it is of interest to know something about the places where these ideas saw the light of day, something about the customs and mores they were founded on, something about the spirit and character of the nations that sanctioned them. It is of interest to study to what extent that spirit, those mores, those practices, have been altered or preserved; to find out what may have been the influences of climate, the effects of government, the causes of customs; in a word, to judge by present conditions what things were like in the past.[1]

Undeniably, there was no dirth of written material in that part of Africa. Let us note, however, that not everyone agrees about including this material in the traditional field of African culture. To those who object, one can reply that Egypt was not the only African region where works of culture were conceived in the written form.

1. C. F. Volney, *Voyage en Syrie et en Égypte (1783–85)*, Paris, Desenne, [1787].

Honorat Aguessy

On examination one discovers that the use of the written word was popular elsewhere. Such is the case in the States of the 'Niger loop civilization', where the Targui, the Moor, the Fulani, the Songhai and the Mandingo peoples rubbed shoulders. The works of the Arab scholars Ibn Khaldun,[1] Ibn Batuta,[2] and others, as well as those of Sudanese scholars like Es-Saadi[3] and Kati Mohammed[4] abound in details about not only the economic life but also the cultural influence of that region.

The world-wide intellectual reputation of the university of Timbuktu between the tenth and the sixteenth centuries is one of the most outstanding instances of that cultural influence. As I. Kaké and Sissoko write, first,

the Sudanese scholars of the African 'Middle Ages' were of the same intellectual class as their Arab colleagues, and sometimes they were even superior, as Abderrahmann El Temini, of the Hedjas, who had been brought to Mali by Kankan Moussa, had occasion to note; [secondly] the term university must be understood in the general and mediaeval sense, that is to say, as the totality of all centres of study and teaching including all the fields of knowledge existing at the time.

For that matter, Timbuktu enjoyed an exceptional intellectual life. In this city of between 70,000 and 80,000 inhabitants, there numbered (according to Sissoko, who bases himself on a passage in the *Tarikh el Fettach*)[5] between 15,000 and 20,000 Koranic students attending some 150 to 180 Koranic schools. Timbuktu's outstanding cultural lustre contributed to the development of scholars whose mastery of science, literature, law, etc., was recognized and admired throughout the world. One can even cite names of intellectuals

1. Ibn Khaldun, *Histoire des Berbères et des Dynasties Musulmanes de l'Afrique Septentrionale*, Vol. 2 (French translation by Baron Slade), Alger, Imprimerie du Gouvernement, 1854.
2. Ibn Batuta, *Voyage dans le Soudan* (French translation by M. Mac Guckin de Slane), Paris, 1843.
3. Abderrahman Ben Abdallah Ben 'Imran Ben Amir Es-Sa'di', *Tarikhes Sudan* (French translation by O. Houdas), Paris, Maisonneuve, 1964 (Unesco Collection of Representative Works, African series).
4. Mahmoud Kati Ben El-Hadj El-Motaouakkel Kati, *Tarikh el Fettah* (French translation by O. Houdas and M. Delafosse), Paris, Maisonneuve, 1964 (Unesco Collection of Representative Works, African series).
5. ibid., p. 316.

specializing in the most abstruse and rarefied types of abstract thinking!

I will mention only one figure—Ahmed Baba, whose complete name contains no less than forty words[1] (as we shall see, this name typifies a mode peculiar to oral cultures, a system of pinpointing and situating the individual within his family, genealogy and society). This renowned doctor, writes Sissoko,

> sums up the highest point of Nigerian culture in one person. . . . He is the culmination of the intellectual development of the great Nigerian city, the quintessence of Sudanese civilization at its apogee. He is the finest product of the Sudanese culture, and the Sudanese culture alone, for, unlike the great scholars of the previous generation, Ahmed Baba never studied elsewhere than at Timbuktu. He therefore provides an excellent measure of the Sudanese university in the latter half of the sixteenth century.

Here we already have the answer to one objection, namely that, given the influence of Islam on the civilization of the Niger loop States, the latter cannot really be considered an authentically African culture. I will only remark briefly that, first, no culture develops or flourishes in complete isolation, and secondly, the authenticity of a culture is not determined at the level of the material or materials on which the mind is brought to bear, but at the level of the culture's individual manner of breaking down, qualifying or synthesizing these materials. Authenticity does not mean cultural solipsism; it is a judgement of the special attention that a culture brings to 'things' common to all the world in order to distribute them into the separate classes of 'objects', 'ideas', performative speech, etc.

Islam's contribution to the Sudanese civilization, at the level of the teachings of the prophet Mohammad, is undeniable. But the scholars at the university of Timbuktu were not mere parrots who repeated what their masters had taught them. If the learned Ahmed Baba earned a great reputation by writing some forty treatises of

1. Ahmed Ben Admed ben Ahmed ben Omar ben Mohammed Akit ben Omar ben Ali ben Yahia ben Koutalata ben Bekr ben Nik ben Lak ben Jahia ben Tachta ben Tabkar ben Hiran ben El Badjard ben Omar ben Abou Bekr ben Omar el Larneci (1556–1627).

major importance on grammar, rhetoric, astronomy, law, theology, history, morals, logic, etc., it was because he sensed that the cultural symbiosis which had produced the university of Timbuktu called for a new way of tackling and reformulating old problems. The Sudanese style of scholarship which he illustrates was respected by the greatest scholars of the sixteenth century—Ahmed Baba was the guest of the leading figures of the Marrakesh intelligentsia.

In short, numerous African thinkers over the centuries have consigned the values of their society and the fruits of their own inspiration and scholarship to writing.

Instead of speaking of the civilization of the Niger loop, I might just as easily have dwelt on the great African intellects Tertullian, Origen, Arnobius, Saint Augustine, Saint Cyril of Alexandria, Saint Cyprian, Saint Firmilian, all of whom were products of the cultural area of Africa which was influenced at a very early date by Christianity. Nor should one forget Terence whose privilege it was to utter a truth which every man should heed: '*Homo sum: humani nihil a me alienum puto.*'

Likewise, I could have cited the names of Ethiopian thinkers famous for their written works. But in doing so I would have made criticism easier for those who reduce traditional African culture to something indefinable and forever changing, on a level with their own fantasies and private zones of darkness. Indeed the intellectual development of the scholars just mentioned was strongly centred on the Christian, and especially the Roman, cultural area. By viewing their contributions as an integral part of the traditional African cultural heritage, might we not be giving undue weight to purely geographical considerations?

This raises the question of what exactly is meant by the term 'tradition'. What is traditional in a people's view of the world? Is it that which is relegated to the mummified past? Is it not rather the individual stamp of a people—a permanent character which, when driven out by modernism, always returns massively? Rather than standing for a finished period in the life of a people—its 'having been'—it conveys its present 'being', not in the sense that it defines the essence of a culture, but in so far as, like any translation of a text into another language, it renders that culture's textual style into the idiom of a contemporary context. In this sense, traditional culture is forever emerging, disappearing and reappearing. It is synonymous with activity, not passivity. It is not a passing thing, like modernism. It, and it alone, characterizes a culture and distinguishes it from other cultures. As I have written elsewhere, tradition is not the repetition of identical sequences in different periods, it is not a force of inertia or conservatism invariably resulting in the same physical and mental gestures, an intellectual paralysis preventing innovation.[1]

That being the case, the specificity of Africa's view of the world can be pinpointed in the characteristic aspects of the African mode of perceiving objects and events, which, even in the throes of a demanding, coercive and often superficial modernity, is constantly able to shift, not only from one domain to another but also from one period to another. It reveals itself in the most contemporary behaviour as well as in the most ancient gestures, in the simplest and most deliberate physical occupations as well as in purely intellectual undertakings, in relations between people as well as in individual attitudes.

Let us now examine these areas and periods more closely.

Despite the occasional appearance of African values in written form, it should again be stressed that the fundamental characteristic of African cultures is their orality. Even when writing is used, tradition—of which I have just said that it is synonymous with activity—expresses itself authentically for the mass of Africans orally, and only orally.

Indeed, it is precisely the fact that it has always been more accessible to the masses which explains why orality has prevailed over scripturality in the Niger loop civilization. During the centuries of intensive, internationally recognized and respected intellectual life when the university of Timbuktu shone as a centre of learning, the culture that was based on writing appeared primarily as a minority and urban phenomenon. As true as it is that the great African scholars mastered the different fields of science and contemporary knowledge, the masses remained content with the oral aspect of everyday cultural life. The very advanced culture of the scholars remained strictly purist from the linguistic point of view: only Arabic, the language of the Koran, could be used to express truth.

1. Honorat Aguessy, 'Tradition Orale et Structures de Pensée: Essai de Méthodologie', *Cahiers d'Histoire Mondiale*, Paris, Unesco, Vol. XIV, No. 2, p. 269–97.

Lacking popular support, this brilliant cultural life soon collapsed.

It should be noted in passing that the continued influence of an élitist culture based on the written word requires a substantial economic base. Deprived of the important Teghazza salt mine, which was coveted by Morocco, deprived of the gold from the Bambouk, Boure and Bito mines (which was for centuries 'probably one of the decisive weapons of Western Islam'), the Sudanese culture which had developed within the framework of writing suddenly vanished. Thus the 'dawn of the modern age in Europe—the sixteenth century—was also the twilight of the civilization of Black Africa', the latter, with the generation of Ahmed Baba, having given the highest promise of world-wide influence.

In any event, in seeking to understand the world view of traditional African culture, it is useful, on the level of methodology, to consult the works of and about the above period. But a number of traps have to be avoided. One of them consists in the retrospective fallacy of picturing the cultural level being analysed in the light of the present state of the same region—though Africans have as much cause as anyone to know that (as Valéry said), 'we civilizations know that we are mortal'.

The retrospective fallacy also makes one tend to overlook the context of economic prosperity which stimulated cultural exchange and was responsible in part for the high level of culture in the Niger loop. Hubert Deschamps writes,

camel caravans crossed the Sahara to Western Sudan to fetch gold (from the Bambouk, Boure and Bito mines), ivory, skins and slaves. They brought salt from the Sahara (Idjil, Teghazza, Bilma) and the products of North Africa—corn, dates, horses, silk and wool garments, copper, silver, glassware. Arab-Berber merchants lived in the Sudan. One route crossed Mauritania, another led to the Niger loop, a third linked Ghadames or Tripoli with Aïr or Chad. These commercial activities doubtless played a part in the birth of the first black kingdoms of the Sudan around the eighth and ninth centuries.[1]

Another trap consists in believing that an oral culture never uses a system of inscription for aiding memory. As I have already pointed

1. Hubert Deschamps, *L'Afrique des Origines à 1945*, p. 348.

out, orality refers to the predominantly oral mode of communication; it does not mean exclusively oral communication arising from a hypothetical incapacity for writing. Orality is the effect as well as the cause of a certain type of social being. It defines specific social relationships by stressing certain factors of social stratification and differentiation (the possession of words of power, the initiation into knowledge which constitutes a sort of guaranteed minimum level of knowledge qualifying the individual).

This being the case, the different areas to investigate in order to define Africa's cultural distinctiveness range from the sphere of religion to that of the most commonplace everyday things. They can be organized as follows: (a) African religious practices; (b) artistic productions: sculpture, architecture, urban design, clothing, etc.; (c) the use and transformation of nature; (d) oral literature: sayings, proverbs, maxims, riddles, tales, legends, myths; (e) games.

I do not intend to undertake an exhaustive and detailed investigation of all the areas in which the African world view is expressed and concretized. Instead I will limit myself to a more modest discussion of some examples of the African peoples' attitudes towards the universe, life and society.

GAMES

Let us begin with a topic that is usually neglected by specialists and experts, who, owing to their training and prejudices, are blind to what it can teach about a society's mentality. I mean games.

One game in particular confirms the relevance of talking about the unity of African views. Based on a number of common principles, it has variants which concretize and add meaning to them. This is the game which some Europeans have called the 'African bowl game', and whose native names, varying from one society to the next, are certainly more meaningful. The Dahomans and Togolese call it '*aji*'; in Abyssinia the name is '*gamada*'; in Senegal it is '*ouri*'; the Masai call it '*dodoi*'; and in Zaire and perhaps all of Central and Eastern Africa it is known as '*mankala*'.[1]

---

1. The game is usually played by two players, each having a row of six bowls containing four seeds or small pebbles each. 'Although there are forms of the game which can be played by more than two players, in which case three or

Honorat Aguessy

Played throughout Africa, this game belongs to the category of games of calculation. Its pan-African character caused one of the first foreigners to mention it to call it 'the national game of Africa'.[1] It is indeed national, and this fact surely connotes a fundamental similarity in outlook among those who play it. Thus one student has written:

Comparison between the Euro-Asian games of calculation and *mankala* has shown that the principal difference between them lies in the fact that each has its own type of preferential counting as regards its major components—board and pieces.

In the Euro-Asian games, the piece values are hierarchical and the board values uniform, whereas in mankala it is the other way round. These two types of counting are explained by a preferential choice . . . Mankala's integration within the social context has resulted in relationships being established between the different languages (in the broadest sense of that word), whereas the Euro-Asian games are considered solely from the historical and etymological points of view.[2]

With communication theory in mind the author adds:

It appears indeed that *Mankala* can usefully shed light on the structure of verbal communication exhibited in the literary works of African societies . . . The communicative function of texts in the oral traditions seems to prevail over their expressive function.

This attempt at theorization shows that games constitute a far from negligible tool for pinpointing the salient features of a society's mentality.

At all events, whereas Marcel Griaule, who observed this game among the Dogon, paid attention particularly to its educational

four rows of bowls are used, the ordinary game is played by two players on a board with two rows of bowls, one for each of the two players. Generally six bowls are used (but sometimes five, seven or eight). When there is no board, the players very often dig out two rows of holes in the ground. In each bowl are placed four pieces: pebbles of the same size, or seeds, or cowries, small shells which formerly served as money. In every case the pieces are moved in the same way.' (Joseph Boyer, in *Présence Africaine*, No. 7, 1949, p. 311.)

1. Stewart Culin, *Mancala, the National Game of Africa*, 1896. (In: U.S. National Museum, *Annual Report 1894*, Washington, 1896.)

2. Unpublished working paper, Laboratoire d'Anthropologie Sociale, Paris.

aspect ('the child acquires the feeling and eventually the idea of quantity in handling the stones used in the game'), and whereas another observer noted that in Dahomey 'the highly complicated combinations of this game require a great deal of concentration', I wish to stress the sociological significance of the fact that this game of calculation, far from being restricted to an élite, is by and large the favourite game of the African masses.

It is a game which does not necessarily have a winner, unlike most games in other countries around the world which always require a winner and a loser. Thus the African game does not inevitably result in one side gaining something and the other side losing it. Considered as an agonistic activity, the game does not depend from start to finish on the elimination of an unlucky opponent. It is the opposite of those parlour games studied by Claude Lévi-Strauss, who writes that their purpose

appears to be disjunctive: they create a differential gap between individual players or sides that nothing designated initially as being unequal. And yet at the end of the game, the participants are divided into winners and losers.[1]

In *mankala*—'the national game of Africa'—the equal status of the players at the beginning of each game (that is to say, the equal number of seeds held by each player) remains unchanged at the end of the game. The actual outcome is of little importance. In principle, this equality is a postulate. The lesson to be learned by examining *mankala* or '*aji*' might be even more valuable if compared with the findings of other studies of African games.

Games themselves do not produce their own theories. The student can only ponder over their rules or compare them with the sayings or proverbs which allude to the principle of games in general. Thus the Fon (Fo in Dahomey) say *mê ji je mê ji je we ayihû nô vivi*, the game is meaningful only in so far as each player in turn participates in it—a sentence which reflects the characteristic quality of understatement in African discourse. Here, it is not only the alternating nature of the game which is being alluded to, but also and

1. Claude Lévi-Strauss, *La Pensée Sauvage*, p. 46, Paris, Plon, 1962.

above all its character of reciprocity and equality. In other words, each player must benefit from the game. No one is to be reduced to the role of the winner's audience.

This raises the question what kind of benefit does the player enjoy. But this is not the place to enlarge on that point. Suffice it to say that there is no transfer of material wealth whatsoever. Perhaps the benefit lies simply in the release of surplus energy, or perhaps it has something to do with ritual—ritual whose effects on both the individual and the group are multiple and as yet not fully explained.

Whatever the case, the fact remains that by examining games we can gain an insight into Africa's view of the world; for games provide a concrete expression of a given attitude towards the universe, life and society, either as a direct outcome of daily behaviour or as a compensation for it.

PROVERBS

Let us now proceed to another area which can provide us with information about the view of the world in Africa—proverbs, sayings and maxims.

Every African society is a treasure-trove of such expressions. Not only is every nation in Africa becoming increasingly aware of their value and systematically collecting them, but also much is being done at the international level to make them known throughout the world.

Why is so much attention being given to what some people consider as inferior products of the intellect? Primarily because what we have here are not works of secondary importance, but excellent ,distillations' of lengthy and mature reflection—the results of experience confirmed a thousand times over. Their anonymous character is simply an indication of how deeply they are embedded in collective life and experience, and to what an extent they are the result of adjustments and testings made by many generations. These laconic expressions, which condense countless individual experiences of society, life and the universe, are generally not self-evident. For this reason, instead of offering a selection of African proverbs, I prefer to dwell on the following points.

To begin with, one would do well, in connection with this or that proverb relating to social, moral or political behaviour, to consider the social group in which the thought emerged and crystallized. For it should not be forgotten that these proverbs cannot always be taken as expressions of ageless universal wisdom. Some of them, it is true, are encountered in all countries at all periods. Others, on the contrary, reflect the peculiar attitude of a given social group within a given country or group of countries. For that matter, Africa (unless it is regarded as the materialization of a fantasy view of social relations eternally characterized by unanimity) is no more a land of miraculous and unbroken understanding among all citizens than is any other part of the world.

Next, whenever the same idea is expressed in a variety of languages and in a variety of countries, it seems useful to collect and compare the different sayings which distil it. A particularly interesting example of what I mean is A. O. Sanda's compilation of proverbs on different themes[1]—patience considered as a virtue, honesty considered as a virtue, gratitude and ingratitude, co-operation and reciprocity in human relations, ignorance, lack of information, experience considered as the best school, leadership, respect for old people, the wisdom and discretion that is expected of the old, the self-respect that is expected of the old, representations, the force of gravity, hope and perseverance, the 'boomerang' effect (as you sow, so shall you reap, etc.).

The main point to be noted about the proverbs from different African societies, is the sense of unity of African thought which they display. At their level of intellectual formulation, and considering their special mode of expression, this unity should be conceived of not as a repetition of identical images and words, but as a dynamic process of metaphorization indicative of the creativity of each different group.

Although they are not repetitious or monotonous in their choice of terms and figures, these 'distillations' of thought are similar in style. For instance, the fundamental antithesis *up/down* is used to express inevitability in Yoruba, Hausa and Ashanti, though in each case in very different words.

---

1. A. O. Sanda, unpublished working paper, delivered at the Symposium International sur l'Autocompréhension Culturelle des Nations, Innsbruck, Austria, July, 1974.

Honorat Aguessy

More strikingly, in the group of proverbs on the self-respect that is expected of the old, different images serve to convey the same idea. The Yoruba say an old man must not make a laughing stock of himself. The corresponding Fo, Kikuyu and Ashanti expressions are: an old man must not lower himself to the level of a child; the Council elders do not leap across streams; when an old man gobbles up all his food, he must clear his own table. These four images are not repetitious, and yet there is no doubt as to the identity or similarity of the thought which they express.

In short, unity of thought does not mean repetition of the same intellectual or physical gestures, or the same images; it expresses a common dynamic mentality which, when confronted with similar problems or situations, produces similar thoughts. That is the reason why proverbs can give a glimpse of the Africans' view of the world.

I might observe incidentally that what is involved here is more than a view: it is really a conception, a balanced conception, which is adapted to the ends and means a given society assigns itself. This is the basis on which the most convincing work on the African conception of the world is being done today.

At this point a question arises: are we dealing with a passing fad, or does this attempt to collect and analyse African proverbs have a solid scholarly basis? A more detailed examination can be made by restricting one's observations to a single country. Let us therefore consider the case of Senegal. According to the available information Senegalese proverbs have been collected for well over a century. In *Fables Sénégalaises* (1828), Roger Le Baron[1] recorded and organized a number of fables, and in *Esquisses Sénégalaises*, another writer, Boilat,[2] gives us a large selection of proverbs.

Boilat even mentions the names of 'certain ancient [Wolof] philosophers'. About the Wolofs in general he writes:

their conversation turns mainly on the proverbs of certain ancient philosophers, . . . on riddles and fables. The history of their philosophers is too interesting to pass over in silence. Their most remarkable philosopher was Cothi-Barma. One could write a long book about the latter's witty sayings.[3]

1. Roger Le Baron, *Fables Sénégalaises*, 1828.
2. Abbé P. D. Boilat, *Esquisses Sénégalaises*, Paris, P. Bertrand, 1853.
3. Boilat, op. cit., p. 345–6.

Traditional African views and apperceptions

Boilat was impressed by the Wolof's style of communication and expression, and noted some of their most striking stories. Here is one of them:

Cothi had left four tufts of hair on his son's head (it being the Wolof custom to shave their children's heads). 'Each of these tufts', he said, 'stands for a moral truth known only to me and to my wife'. As for his wife, she had a son from a previous marriage, but his head was shaved like those of other children. Mightily intrigued by the riddle of the tufts, the Demel (i.e. the chief or king) sought for a long time to discover its meaning, but in vain. Then he summoned the philosopher's wife and bribed her with presents.

'The first tuft means that a king is neither a relative nor a protector. The second tuft means that a child born of a previous marriage is not a son but a cause of civil disturbance. The third tuft means that one should love one's wife but not trust her entirely. The fourth tuft means that a country needs an old man.'[1]

... Condemned to death by the king, who had been angered by the first symbol, but later saved from execution by an old man who had a great deal of influence over the king, Cothi was brought before the latter, to whom he explained calmly: 'Is it not true that a king is neither a relative nor a protector, since, owing to a secret which I did not reveal to you and which I was fully entitled to keep to myself, you condemned me to death, forgetting both the services I have rendered you and the enduring friendship that has bound us together since childhood?

'Is it not true that one should love one's wife without trusting her entirely, since my wife, to whom I had confided my secret for the sole purpose of testing her trustworthiness, has betrayed it for base gifts?

'Is it not true that a child born of a previous marriage is not a son but a source of civil disturbance, since, when he should have been bewailing his father who had been condemned to death, his only thought on the contrary was to ask me for clothes which he feared he might lose?

'Is it not true finally that a country needs an old man, for had it not been for a wise and prudent old man whose weighty arguments curbed your fury, I should no longer be alive at this moment, but dead, a victim of your unjust anger?'[2]

1. ibid., p. 352.
2. ibid., p. 354–5.

Honorat Aguessy

Boilat notes that 'more than five thousand adages or maxims are attributed to Cothi'. From another Wolof 'philosopher', Masseni, Cothi's grandson, he quotes the following four adages:

1. He who despises his condition is a man without honour.
2. When a son is restless beneath his father's roof, it is because his mother is impatient.
3. The poor man who fears the sun, fears a relative (a benefactor).
4. He who enters another's house to beg for alms is wrong; the owner took pains to build it.

Lastly, in the sketch that he gives of a third Wolof philosopher, Biram Thiam-Demba, Boilat describes another type of expression peculiar to oral cultures—riddles, which he associates particularly with social gatherings. He writes:

This man concerned himself with riddles for no other purpose than to amuse the idle. Nevertheless, the people of Cayor praise his wit highly. In the evening, by moonlight or by an open fire, the Wolofs gather together and with great shrieks of laughter assail each other with questions and answers, all of them invented by this philosopher.

. . . Each person in turn asks a riddle. When someone has guessed the right answer, there are shouts from all sides: *Wenc neu dug!* (He speaks the truth). If the riddle seems particularly difficult, they all hold their chins and exclaim, *Bissimilay Dhiame!* (In the name of the God of truth).[1]

Boilat makes an interesting observation about the different categories of proverb. According to him, the Wolofs have two sorts of saying: the trinitarian proverb and the ordinary proverb. The trinitarian proverb involves three things, objects or thoughts. For instance: three things are necessary in this world—friends, face and bags of money. Or, three things are to be preferred in this world: possession, power and knowledge. Or again, three things are better than all others in this world: health, being on good terms with one's neighbours and being universally loved.

The ordinary proverbs include every type of saying: 'A sassy tongue is a bad weapon', or 'It is better to know oneself for what

---

1. Boilat, op. cit., p. 354–5.

one is than to learn it from others', or 'Too many questions make a man indiscreet'.

Boilat's work shows us that the awareness of the value of proverbs considered as expressions of the Africans' view of the world is by no means a recent phenomenon. Perhaps that is so because the first foreigners to take an interest in African sayings had no doctrine, no 'school of thought' to defend, and were simply content to describe things which impressed them and which they found to be of value. Even today, few men of African culture overlook the rich field of proverbs when seeking to understand their own society.

ART

Having taken a look at games and proverbs, and having seen how useful they can be in the context of the present study, let us briefly consider art.

Whether it be in sculpture and carved figures whose purity and rigour of design testify to a high aesthetic level sustained by deep reflection, or in architecture, urban design, choreography, music, or simply plaiting hair, the African attitude towards the universe, life and society expresses itself not in speculative form but in the manner of a creative and liberating social activity.

Erwin Panofsky has brilliantly analysed the relationship between Gothic architecture and scholastic thinking.[1] I see no reason why, in the study of cultures not centred on written treatises, it should not likewise be possible to identify, for example in the work of the builders of the giant Bamileke houses (Benin), or the conical Chadian houses or the Somba castles (northern Benin), the under-lying intellectual attitudes and ideas about social relations which those structures embody.

The African artefact belongs to a world whose unity, disclosed by multiple levels of contrasts, constitutes a major aspect of the integration of human activities within a dynamic culture.

In his analysis of Kabyle houses, Pierre Bourdieu has already succeeded in demonstrating the social thinking reflected in their

---

1. Erwin Panofsky, *Architecture Gothique et Pensée Scolastique*, French translation by P. Bourdieu. Paris, Éditions de Minuit, 1967.

subtle architecture. Studies of the same kind should be extended to the oral cultures. They will show how, despite the lack of written treatises, one can nevertheless recognize man in his concrete life, the whole man and the whole of life, in the expressive designs of the artist-craftsman.

RELIGION

The primary importance of religion, as compared with games, proverbs and art, is undeniable in understanding the specificity of Africa's traditional views and apperceptions.

African religion, in a sense, is both the cause and the effect of oral civilization.[1] Religion functions as a living substitute for books recording collective experience. The African religious practices express and preserve the African man's relationship to the world. In their prescriptions and prohibitions, their definitions of what is lawful or forbidden, these practices concretize the values and countervalues of African society.

The religious domain is an exceedingly rich one. Limiting ourselves to those aspects of religion which shed light on the present topic, let us begin by observing that African religion includes, among other things, veritable 'schools' of training, not only for the faithful but also for ordinary citizens. These 'schools' consist in what is generally called *initiation*.

Apart from the 'school' of day-to-day family and social life which enhances the individual's experience, initiation constitutes a vital institution for teaching and training the citizen. It is through it that the citizen accedes to the vegetable, mineral, animal and human categories established in each society's vocabulary. It is by means of initiation that the citizen advances beyond the ordinary knowledge of his society's values to an understanding of the why and wherefore of things. The citizen who has been initiated is no longer a drifter (an *ahè*, as the Fo say) but a complete, fully-rounded man who understands how values and institutions are produced, and perhaps also where their origin lies.

1. cf. H. Aguessy, 'Religions Africaines, comme Effet et Source de la Civilisation de l'Oralité', *Religions Africaines comme Source de Valeurs de Civilisation*, Paris, Présence Africaine, 1972.

The attempt to explain origins is made within myths (speech, for example), which are not false narratives or narratives meant to deceive others; rather, they constitute the fundamental discourse underlying all explanations of the social order and counter-order. Thus the man who has been admitted to the secrets or revelations of initiation is no longer a walking dummy; the Fo say of him, for example, that his 'ear is pierced' (*e t òto*).

But initiation—a ceremony of limited duration—does not disclose all knowledge. The individual's schooling is continued by a moral, scientific and political development which time alone provides, and provides only to the man who perseveres. It demands a sustained effort amounting to a life style, an attitude towards life, society and the universe which cannot be reduced to a few formulas and prescriptions. For that reason I would say that the knowledge imparted in initiation is of a qualitative, not a quantitative order: it is a matter of learning how to live well, not of accumulating facts.

The above remarks might be completed by the observations of a number of scholars. Writing about the Koumen, for example, A. Hampaté Bâ and G. Dieterlen declare that

Initiation is knowledge—knowledge of God and of the rules that He has established; knowledge of one's self, for initiation appears as an ethical teaching too; knowledge, also, of all that is not God.[1]

Furthermore this 'science' must become universal; each of its elements and aspects must constitute a part of the whole. The Fulani say: 'One does not know everything. All that one knows is a part of everything.' 'Initiation', goes another Fulani saying, 'begins when one enters the corral and ends in the grave'.

To understand this last aphorism one must know that

the life of a Fulani as an initiated herdsman begins with his entrance into the corral and ends with his formal exit from it, which takes place when he reaches the age of 63. It comprises three periods, each lasting 21 years: 21 years of apprenticeship, 21 years of practising his herding trade and 21 years of teaching.

Leaving the corral is a kind of death for the herdsman. He then calls

1. A. Hampaté Bâ and G. Dieterlen, *Koumen*, Paris, Mouton, 1961.

Honorat Aguessy

his successor—his own son, or else the most qualified and devoted of the initiates. The newcomer sucks the old man's tongue, for saliva is considered the vehicle of the *word*, that is to say, of knowledge; then the old man whispers in the young man's ear the secret name of the cattle.[1]

A little further, the authors give an interesting detail:

There are 33 grades for the 33 phonemes of the Fulani language, plus three higher grades which are inaudible—those of the 'unspoken' but ever-present word, or the 'word for the unknown'.[2]

This account gives one an idea of the essential role which initiation plays as a 'school' for educating each citizen, not only by teaching him the technical rudiments of his trade, but also by instructing him about the organization of the universe, and about what man can hope for in life and is capable of doing.

This form of education is praised in a Basa text (Cameroon), which incidentally outlines a number of ideas about the Basa conception of man:

Man is like a tree: he is born upright, and bends later under the pressure of the winds of the world. Just like a tree, he can be straightened out when he is still young. But just as an old twisted trunk can no longer be straightened out, so it is difficult to straighten out a depraved adult. A child is born free of all vice. However his innocence gradually disappears as he grows and learns. After he becomes aware of himself, he discovers the world which surrounds him and affects him. Out of curiosity and a taste for adventure, he very soon discovers evil. At this age he has not yet been warned about anything. It is the duty of his elders, who have experienced life before him, to instruct him so that he may eschew evil and seek out good. The teacher is both a referee and a trainer. He himself is not necessarily a good player. But he knows all the rules of the game, and thus he can teach them to others and compel others to abide by them.[3]

The moral teaching imparted to the pupil by the experienced adult acquires its full significance as a set of pronouncements to be honoured and obeyed only within the framework of religious prac-

1. ibid., p. 19.
2. ibid.
3. Basa popular song.

tices in which all things partake of the sacred. It is for this reason that the student of African culture will uncover mines of ideas on traditional views and apperceptions in the religious domain. By studying the theologies and cosmologies worked out by the various circles of initiates, he will learn (as Marcel Griaule did) that Dogon 'knowledge', for example, consists of

22 categories of 12 elements each, that is, 264 elements, each one of which heads a list of 22 couples . . . this system of 11,616 signs symbolizes all beings and all possible situations seen from the male point of view (with a corresponding system of the same magnitude for women).

One discovers also that the Dogon and other Africans

have developed an indigenous explanation for the different aspects of nature (anthropology, botany, zoology, astronomy, anatomy and physiology) and social phenomena (social, religious and political structures, techniques, arts, economics, etc.).[1]

Other characteristics of the Africans' conception of the universe, life and society are revealed by religious practices. Thus the treatment of the body, which serves to express the relationship between man and the divine, proves the inadequacy of dualistic religious thought, which tends to eliminate the body in order to concentrate exclusively on the spirit. Bodily techniques are of utmost significance in Africa where it is thought that divinity expresses itself through the body.

For that matter, African divinity is not just something to be demonstrated in the arguments of theological schools; nor is it the conclusion of a syllogism. It is a manifestation acted out in collective rejoicing. In the unity of body and spirit, individual and community, worship and rejoicing, veneration and familiarity, it is expressed by the whole man, the man linked to society, accepting and sublimating everything that makes him a man.

One further point calls for comment here—namely, the variety of names by which an African God is called. Those who are forever on the lookout for polytheism everywhere except in Europe are often misled by this multiplicity of divine names, seeing in it nothing

1. M. Griaule and G. Dieterlen, *Le Renard Pâle*, p. 40, Paris, Institut d'Ethnologie, 1965.

more than a confirmation of their preconceived ideas. By situating this mode of addressing divinity within the context of oral culture, one gets a better understanding of that practice.

Indeed the proliferation of names for a being—whether human or divine—is an indication of its importance. When a child is born, he is given a secret name and an ordinary name; later he is assigned other names to mark important stages in his life. The large number of names given to an individual expresses his parents' expectations for him, his own expectations, his mythical connection with the collective ancestors, his position in his family, the manner in which he was born (head first, feet first, with his umbilical cord around his neck, etc.), and his idiosyncrasies. The large number of divine names must be understood in the same context. The best way of praising the glory and might of God or divinity is to give Him or it several names. Thus divinity is not demonstrated, but named. Any study of the multiplicity of divine names that concludes with some generalization about polytheism is thus on the wrong track.

MYTHS

As I wrote above, myths are not lies, false species of discourse intended to deceive, but the very foundation of all explanations of the social order and counter-order.

Having discussed religion, I take up this examination of myths because the two fields are not unrelated. In this connection, one must take care in distinguishing between the different categories of narrative. Indeed, those who use the terms 'fable', 'tale', 'legend' and 'myth' interchangeably are in no position to appreciate the specific status of myths or to understand the insights which they can offer into the traditional African views and apperceptions of the world.

Léopold Sédar Senghor has tried to bring some order to this indiscriminate use of terms for the different categories of narrative. Unfortunately he has analysed only the differences between tales and fables. In his view, a tale is a narrative in which animals are not given active roles, whereas a fable uses animals as its principal actors. One would have liked to know under what conditions Léopold Senghor would suggest using the term *myth*. One wonders, furthermore, whether the distinction he makes between tale and fable is operative in the African context. Is the criterion of the presence or absence of animals decisive in Africa? Are there not other criteria—such as the time of day, or night, when a story is told?

The conceptual analysis of the words 'fable', 'tale', 'legend' and 'myth' as they occur in the European context constitutes a blind alley for our purposes. We must avoid it and, instead, take a look at the words which designate the different categories of narrative in African terminology.

In Boilat's book,[1] published well over a century ago, we read the following:

The Wolofs call proverbs, maxims, adages, riddles and fables by the same name, *Laibe*, because one can draw a moral lesson from them all.

It is usually in the evening, by moonlight, at the doorway of their huts or seated on the sand in the middle of the village square, that the Wolofs like to tell fables.

The story-teller is placed in the centre of the circle; he uses every device to amuse his listeners; bringing in men and animals, he imitates their gestures, their expressions and their voices; from time to time he sings, and the assembly repeats the refrain amidst a great clapping of hands, accompanied by a tom-tom . . . The story-teller never draws the moral; it is up to the listeners to reach their own conclusion.

Here too, one would have liked to know what word the Wolofs of those times used for 'myth'.

Let us now turn to an African cultural area in which there are more terms for the different types of narrative: the Fo culture (Benin). We find the following terms used in everyday speech: *Xǒ, tà, Xójɔxó, yɛxó, xɛxǒ, glu, huenùxǒ*. What do these terms mean? Numerous definitions have been given by eminent scholars.[2] For the purposes of the present study, I shall attempt to systematize—so as to stress the characteristics of myth—a number of distinctions occurring more or less unsystematically in everyday Fo speech (taken as an example).

1. Boilat, op. cit., p. 391–2.
2. cf. Ahanhanzo Maurice Glélé, *Dânxome*, p. 16–17, Paris, Nubia, 1974.

Honorat Aguessy

Xó apparently means 'history, occurrence, news'; *tà*: 'a true story concerning a family's past'; *Xójɔxó*: 'a datable historical account'; *yɛxó*: 'a fairy-tale'; *glu*: 'a tale, a fable, an anecdote'; *xɛxó*: 'a tale'; *huenùxó* would seem (provisionally) to mean 'a true or legendary story'.[1]

Let us consider these words in terms of their everyday connotations, while asking certain questions, such as, At what time of day is a given type of narrative told? Who recites or relates it? To whom is it related? At what point does the truth or untruth of the narrative become a requirement or a criterion? Using this approach we should be able to arrive at a definition of the myth and its status, and we should be able to discern the kind of lesson that is to be drawn from it.

The native term *huenùxó* apparently is used to designate myths. A myth (*huenùxó*) can be told at any time of the day. On the other hand, it is governed by two restrictions: first, as regards the qualification of the person who receives its message, and secondly, as regards the ability and the authority of the person who delivers and 'reactivates' the message. Thus it is clearly established that not everyone is able to understand the import of the message delivered by the reciter of myths. Furthermore, it appears that the reciter is generally a specialist in religious practices (or at least in divination).

Another characteristic of the *huenùxó* lies in the fact that the concept of true or false is irrelevant to it. Rather it is the principles of authority and effective solidarity between speaker and listener that matter here. The purpose of a myth is to acquaint the believer with an archetypal story so that he can resolve an unsettling existential problem. Within the context of the relationship of effective solidarity, the word is manifested as an act. The myth provides a symbolic framework within which the voice poses the problem of reality as that of an object considered here and now between speaker and listener.

Still another characteristic of the myth (the Fo myth at any event) lies in the fact that the expert does not recite it simply because he enjoys talking or wants to amuse. He expects the listener to grasp the specific lesson of the story and to resolve his personal problem by following the path indicated by it. In other words, the myth acquires

1. cf. Segulora Fon-French dictionary.

significance to the extent that the listener-questioner is governed by the conclusions reached by the narrative.

Such is the *huenùxǫ́*, as distinguished (in a variety of ways) from the *tà* (historico-mythical narratives), the *yɛxó* (fairy-tales), the *glu* (anecdotes pertaining to any aspect of life), etc.

Though all these forms of narrative have a common basis in the spoken word, the *huenùxǫ́* alone, it should be emphasized, depends entirely on the spoken word for its effectiveness.

In this context one cannot help recalling Pavlov, who believed that the spoken word

interacts with all the external and internal stimuli reaching the cerebral hemispheres; it acts as a signal for them and replaces them. For this reason it can induce the same reactions as those produced by those same stimuli.[1]

The conjunction of voice, gesture and rhythm confers upon the spoken word of the teller of the myth—as well as upon the word (i.e. the message) delivered by the narrative—such power and such prestige that the myth (*huenùxǫ́*)[2] has, in a sense, nothing in common with the mere entertainment value of the other forms of narrative adumbrated in native theory.

To put this idea somewhat differently, let me say that the African myth (even when its effectiveness is disguised under a cloak of commonplace speech, in much the same way that the sages who tell the myths conceal their power and knowledge 'within the folds of the rags they are dressed in') pertains to the order of symbolic expression.

This order, as I understand it, is distinguished from the order of images (*l'imaginaire*) and the order of things (*le réel*), to use the terminology of the Freudian school of Paris.

Jacques Lacan, the leader of this psycho-analytical school, defines the order of symbolic expression (*le symbolique*) as that which gives meaning to the order of images and the order of things. To the extent that a mental configuration is not specific, that it is not a determinant with respect 'to the structure or the dynamics of a process', one can speak of the 'autonomy of the order of symbolic

1. I. P. Pavlov, 'Derniers Résultats des Recherches sur le Travail des Hémisphères Cérébraux', *Journal de Psychologie*, 1926.
2. For fuller details see my thèse d'état, Paris, Sorbonne, 1973.

expression', of the 'ascendency of the order of symbolic expression' over the order of images and the order of things, indeed of the 'supremacy of the order of symbolic expression' over that of images.[1]

The order of symbolic expression is the order or constituent organization, the chain which imprisons man 'already prior to his birth' and continues 'until after his death'. It is coercive and permanent compared with the order of images which consists of the successive forms or ordinary and impermanent expressions of the order of symbolic expression giving rise to the order of things.

In the light of this trilogy of ideas, which may prove useful for locating the category of narrative into which the myth (*huenùxó*) falls—as distinguished from the other categories (*tà, glu, xẹxó*, etc.), it seems to me that the primordial character of myths—giving meaning to the realities of everyday life, as well as to the contents of the other forms of discourse—needs to be particularly emphasized here. Moreover it is on the strength of this character that the mythical domain can be linked to the religious, in the context of a primarily oral culture whose foremost social values are surrounded by an aura of religiosity.

A great number of divinatory narratives pertaining to the creation of the world, to the establishment of order, to man's status in the universe, to this or that moral principle and how it is justified, to the different areas and aspects of society, to the best way of living one's life, etc., can all be called myths according to the logic of this analysis. All of them belong to a level of discourse above and beyond any possible intent to deceive on the part of the narrator, insofar as he is integrated in the order explained by these narratives, just as the listener is.

The African myth, therefore, is not a form of narrative which sets out deliberately to deceive. Considering the variety of themes which it entertains, I would say that, on the level of the spoken word, it delivers the key ideas governing the African conception of the world. As such it can be compared with the other areas of our investigation—games, architecture, riddles, proverbs and fables (and with still other areas I have not touched on, such as music, choreography and urban design).

1. J. Lacan, *Écrits*, p. 11, 52, 468, 546, Paris, Éditions du Seuil, 1966.

Now in all of these areas, there is one common permanent feature: the verbal, gestural, artistic or recreational understatement, or more exactly semi-statement.

In every case the type of discourse which vehicles thought does not continue uninterrupted to a full elucidation of its implicit meaning. Instead it calls for the active participation of an interlocutor, or of an observer or listener. In myth, despite the length of the narrative, it seeks to 'conceal from the uninitiated a precious granule of—so it appears—valid universal knowledge'. Proverbs on the contrary, despite their condensed character, reveal everything to the interlocutor, causing him at the same time to participate in their teaching. Even when it is acted out or uttered spontaneously, the semi-statement tells us much about the essential principles of the society we are studying. It is a society in which life and the universe could not conceivably be shouldered by the isolated individual reduced to solipsism. The 'other' is always implicit; it is always called upon within the framework of that which conditions and perhaps even determines the 'I' and the 'we' together: I mean the anteriority, or at the very least the simultaneity, of the community whenever the 'I' is asserted.

It is this anteriority which finds itself theorized in the primordial language of myth.

It is far more instructive to extract from the different fields mentioned here the traditional African views and apperceptions than to examine the statements and states of mind of this or that scholar affirming or denying the existence of an African philosophy.

When all is said and done, are not all philosophies composed of more or less clearly articulated views and apperceptions expressing the imagination of an individual or a group?

If one can legitimately accept the interpretations of the world —often brilliant but sometimes wayward—which society is encumbered with as it strives to transform the world, can one not just as legitimately acknowledge the ways of thinking which are actively engaged in transforming the world and constantly present in the various activities of everyday life? Logic and thought follow many paths. In order to attend and to respond to each one of them, we must take care to avoid lazy dogmatisms of any kind.

Honorat Aguessy

BIBLIOGRAPHY

ABRAHAM, W. E. *The Mind of Africa*. London, Weidenfeld & Nicolson, 1962.

AGUESSY, H. La Religion Africaine Comme Effet et Source de la Civilisation de l'Oralité. Paris, Présence Africaine (Colloque de Cotonou 1970), 1972.

———. Tradition Orale et Structures de Pensée, Essai de Méthodologie. *Cahiers d'Histoire Mondiale*, Vol. XIV, No. 2, Paris, Unesco, 1972.

———. Le Choc des Cultures. De la Technique-médiation à la Technique-aliénation. *Axes*, Vol. V/1, Paris, 1972.

———. *Essai sur le Mythe de Legba*. Paris, Sorbonne, 1973. (Unpublished thesis.)

BALANDIER, G. *La Vie Quotidienne au Royaume du Kongo*. Paris, Hachette, 1965.

———. *Sens et Puissance*. Paris, Presses Universitaires de France, 1971.

BARRET, Dr P. *Sénégambie et Guinée, La Religion Gabonaise; l'Afrique Occidentale*. Paris, Callamel et Cie., 1888.

BASCOM, W. R. The Myth-ritual Theory. *Journal of American Folklore*, Vol. 70, 1957.

BASTIDE, R. *Les Religions Africaines au Brésil*. Paris, Presses Universitaires de France, 1960.

BOUQUIAUX, L. *Textes Birom (Nigeria septentrional) avec Traduction et Commentaire*. Liège, Université de Liège, 1971.

CAILLOIS, R. *Les Jeux et les Hommes*. Paris, Gallimard, 1958. (Revised 1967.)

CALAME-GRIAULE, G. *Ethnologie et Langage, la Parole Chez les Dogon*. Paris, Gallimard, 1965.

———. Ésotérisme et Organization Sociale au Soudan. *Bulletin de l'IFAN*, Vol. XVI, Series B, No. 34, 1954.

COLIN, R. *Les Contes Noirs de l'Ouest Africain*. Paris, Présence Africaine, 1957.

DELAFOSSE, M. *Civilisation Négro-Africaine*. Paris, Stock, 1925.

DESCHAMPS, H. *Traditions Orales et Archives au Gabon*. Paris, Berger-Levrault, 1962.

DIAGNE, P. Linguistique et Culture en Afrique, *Présence Africaine*, Vol. XLVI, 1963.

DIETERLEN, G. Myth et Organisation Sociale en Afrique Occidentale. *Journal de la Société Africaine* (Paris), Vol. XXIX, No. 1, 1959.

DIOP, Ch. A. *L'Unité Culturelle de l'Afrique Noire*. Paris, Présence Africaine, 1959.

DUCROT, O. *Dire et ne Pas Dire*. Paris, Hermann, 1972.

DUMÉZIL, G. *Mythes et Dieux des Germains*. Paris, Leroux, 1939.

ELIADE, M. *La Nostalgie des Origines, Méthodologie et Histoire des Religions*. Paris, Gallimard, 1971.

EVANS-PRITCHARD, E. E. *Nuer Religion*. Oxford, Clarendon Press, 1956.

FORDE, D. *African Worlds, Studies in the Cosmological Ideas and Social Values of African Peoples*. London, Oxford University Press, 1960.

FOUCAULT, M. *L'Ordre du Discours*. Paris, Gallimard, 1971.

GLÉLÉ, A. M. *Dânxomé*. Paris, Nubia, 1974.

HAZOUME, P. *Doguicimi*. Paris, Larose, 1938.

HOLAS, B. *Les Dieux d'Afrique Noire*. Paris, Librairie Orientaliste, 1968.

HOUIS, M. Littérature de Style Oral. *La Grande Encyclopédie Larousse*, Vol. 2, Paris, Librairie Larousse.

Traditional African views and apperceptions

HOUENOU, T. K. *L'Involution des Métamorphoses et des Métempsychoses de l'Univers*. Paris, 1923.

JAULIN, R. *La Mort Sara*. Paris, Union Générale d'Éditions, 1971.

KAGAME, A. La Littérature Orale au Ruanda. *Les Prêtres Noirs s'Interrogent*. Paris, Éd. du Cerf, 1957.

MAQUET, J. J. *Afrique: Les Civilisations Noires*. Paris, Horizons de France, 1962.

MERCIER, P. *Civilisation du Bénin*. Paris, Société Continentale d'Éditions Modernes Illustrées, 1962.

MBITI, J. S. *Concepts of God in Africa*. London, S.P.C.K., 1970.

N'KRUMAH, K. *Le Consciencisme*. Paris, Payot, 1964.

PAQUES, V. L'Unité de la Pensée Africaine. *Revue de l'Institut de Sociologie*. Paris, 1966.

PAULME, D. Littérature Orale et Comportements Sociaux en Afrique Noire, *L'Homme* (Paris), Vol. I, 1961.

PRICE-MARS, J. *Ainsi Parla l'Oncle*. Paris, Leméac, 1973.

SENGHOR, L. S. Les Fondements de l'Africanité ou Négritude et Arabisme. *L'Unité Africaine* (Dakar), No. 242–4, February 23, March 2, March 9, 1967.

THOMAS, L.-V. *Les Diola*. Dakar, IFAN.

TSHIBANGU, Th. *Le Propos d'une Théologie Africaine Puz*. Kinshasa, 1974.

VANSINA, J. *De la Tradition Orale, Essai sur la Méthode Historique*. Tervuren (Belgique), Musée Royal de l'Afrique Centrale, 1961.

ZAHAN, D. *Religion, Spiritualité et Pensée Africaine*. Paris, Payot, 1970.

African renaissance and cultural issues

Pathé Diagne

Today questions of culture in Africa fall under the issue of cultural renaissance. Since the sixteenth century the African continent has generally lagged far behind the West in technology and the sciences. In these circumstances, African humanism has not been able to evolve a material basis that was efficient enough to safeguard it from foreign hegemony. The wars of liberation have dismantled what remained of the colonial structures raised on the ruins of political and cultural resistance. For almost a century the imperial ethnocentric ideology has put a damper on the national cultures of the continent. It has dictated socio-cultural models shaped from its own point of view with reference to its own interests, its own values, its own languages, its own order; and these models have placed a screen between the people and their institutions, their schools, their economic systems, their view of the world and their very idea of their own history. Hence, Africa's renaissance as a collective undertaking is no different from the similar movements which have blossomed forth periodically in Europe or Asia. It appears primarily as a reconquest of African man's optimum cultural space. It is an attempt to bring culture up to date, to integrate it into modernity. It is a reaction against the cultural imperialisms, especially those of Europe.

The issue of a Black or African renaissance raises three major questions.

Pathé Diagne

What is the meaning, in the contemporary world, of cultural specificity and its modes of expression?

To what extent can the African individual assume an institutional heritage, a conception of the world, a linguistic tradition, an art and a symbolic order? Is it, in fact, in his interest to do so?

What does assuming a tradition's creativity imply? Is the cultural heritage essential to the expression of specificity or originality? In what way does it confer upon the attempt to bring about a renaissance the twofold sense of rediscovery and reference for the enterprise of renewal?

The history of the ideas, movements and theories of any given renaissance makes one thing plain. It is easier to brandish one's past and one's ethical or aesthetic traditions than it is to define a cultural line that is evident to all, an immutable order of values in a profoundly changing world. What trace of Gothic architecture remains in the works of Eero Saarinien or Mies Van der Rohe? What relationship is there between a Tassili rock-painting and a picture by Papa Ibra Taal or the Brazilian artist, Tiberio? Is there anything in the latter's work that recalls the White Lady of Aouanrhet or the gigantic God of Jubharen and that is not found in the fancies of Chagall or the stark lines of Picasso?

Even in a renaissance, the artist's role is to destroy, to break the shackles of tradition so as to release the creative energies and the imagination. The political or moral innovator perceives fruitful flaws in society. He stresses them in order to create a new equilibrium and more generous rules of life, which he descries beyond this or that antiquated custom.

The figurative Ife heads, the geometrical designs of Kuba masks strike our sensibilities. We perceive and understand them with an eye and with feelings which are perhaps no longer those of the artists who gave life to them. To an intellectual of the Maghreb, to a Wolof aesthete or to a New York collector they may disclose a significance that is lost to a Yoruba or Baoulé planter. These works are the landmarks of an experience which is being perpetuated. They do not identify inalterable references.

The traditional oral narrative of the Negro-African story-teller or singer of tales employs a technique of characterization and a mode of dramatization which are developed against the background of a not infrequently simple narrative structure. Occurrences are grafted on to a linear plot. An abundance of adventures creates a constant tension. Paradoxically, the modern novel seems to be following this same path, which might appear to be simplistic in Joyce's wake. Increasingly it is borrowing the by now familiar style of radio and television. Thus the aesthetics of oral expression has renewed the art of fiction. Very likely it will also produce a typically Negro-African art of film. Modern man, whose time has become more and more precious, depends on these media to acquaint him with the great works of the past which, only a century ago, occupied the moments of leisure in agrarian civilizations. This does not necessarily mean that the old techniques have necessarily lost all of their effectiveness.

It is Chinua Achebe's faithful adherence to the Ibo language and mentality—his ability to convey their outlook, their experience, their thought—which gives *Things Fall Apart* and *Arrow of God* their deeply intimate tone. No modern African writer, with the possible exception of the author of *Chaka*, the Bantu novelist Thomas Mafolo, equals him in that respect. Achebe's originality stems from the fact that his work reflects a specific emotional experience, a specific culture and artistic approach. It is strikingly different from the way in which Hemingway, Aragon or Kawabata are original. Achebe makes the world a richer place when he shows us an aspect of man, as seen through the culture, the values, the language, the concepts, the modes of expression and the world-view of Okonkwo and Ikemufa. He appeals to us not only because he has talent, but also because he is different. He introduces us to a set of feelings and to an aesthetics which are not those of an Italian, nor those of a Japanese, nor even those of a neighbouring Yoruba.

One of the peculiarities of the cultural fact is its ambiguity. It is a phenomenon which is simultaneously specific and general. It is a living thing, and has components and follows paths of development which are often contradictory and divergent. Its measure is man. The institution, the ethical or aesthetic view which it underpins, the meanings which it assigns objects, beings, the economy, the relationships between one's self and others or between one's self and objects, acquire a permanent value only in terms of definite choices and contexts. But culture is not just an ambiguous phenomenon. It has a dissentious character. Like nations, cultures establish relationships of power. They serve interests. A cultural, linguistic or institutional heritage constitutes a frame of reference, a means of organization. A foreign language or socio-cultural unit cannot be borrowed with impunity. An ethnic group, a class, a country deliberately adopts given values or a given view of the world insofar as it attains its equilibrium and its autonomy in that view or those values. In one way or another an alien cultural heritage always alienates those who adopt it. Foreign cultural structures claiming to be universal invariably conceal an imperialistic design. It is no accident that renaissances have always been nationalistic reactions, attempts at establishing freedoms, schools, socio-cultural models, political power and an art and a literature which further a specific view of the world.

Negro art and the history of Africa have helped to overcome the alienation of the African individual. In some instances they have rid the non-African of his prejudices. The Negro artist has asserted himself by producing works of a high standard of quality which have exerted a world-wide influence. African history has gained recognition thanks to E. W. Blyden, Ajayi, Chiek Anta Diop, J. Ki Zerbo and Basil Davidson; and thanks, above all, to the independent stands and the successful liberation wars of the African peoples. Already in the early days of Egypt's redis-covery by Europe, Champollion had theorized that the civilization of the pharaohs might have sprung from Negro origins. But this idea gained no more acceptance in its time than did *Nations Nègres*, which was carefully ignored during the colonial period. Today, as Alioune Diop points out in his preface to the catalogue of the 1967 Dakar exhibition, the loudest and often the most authoritative voices to speak about Negro art are European and American, foreign to the African continent.

Studies and the teaching of the Black African, Afro-American and Afro-Arab cultures are flourishing outside of Africa. Only recently Africans were demanding that their contested cultures, history and art be acknowledged. They are so today; they have become famous and have even been integrated into a less conflict-prone world. Africa's cultural contribution is seen not only as something different and original, but also as something that enriches all men. Such has not always been the case. And even now the view which foreigners have of the African cultures and the role which the foreign hegemonies assign to those cultures rob the acceptance of the facts and the change of attitudes of any real significance. In this sense, the African cultural heritage becomes truly significant, in the context of a renaissance, only insofar as it perpetuates itself outside of its texts, its museums and its folklore. Its vocation is that of a creative tradition.

The product of a culture, that is to say the sum total of its institutions, works, arts and writings, constitutes a heritage. This heritage is a given fact, a datum, in a changing world. It may survive or it may die. It may alienate or it may liberate. To the extent that it fulfills that function its contribution remains a vital one.

Samory, El Hadj Omar, the pharaoh Mentuhotep are inspiring, even exemplary figures. But history continues to be made not only with ideas, ideals and cultural references but also with the experience, the actions and the behaviour of those who are living. The wars of liberation must be served by an active Shaka, not just a portrayal of Shaka in the theatre or in the militant paintings of Sokoto. The literary-artistic product of a culture may cease to have an echo. The finished cultural content, that is to say the completed work, is a datum that has been conquered and shared. Beyond whatever pleasure it affords, it continues to be of interest thanks to the cultural life which it acquires.

Sculpture in itself has no existence. Only the form a statue in Ife, Karnak or Nok displays is relevant. From site to site, this form varies; in those variations lies its originality. Specificity expresses a culture's means, its ability to forge its own tools and its own language, its power to assert its own vision, its own hidden, or in any case latent and unique, genius.

To a far greater extent than do cultural nuances or the differences in emotional experience, it is language which gives uniqueness to the various forms of art and humanism, to works and talents. Notions and concepts can be borrowed. On the other hand the apperception which governs the formulation of these concepts within a culture, or the analysis which that culture employs, is rarely transferable. Language characterizes man. Language makes for his originality.

Negro art has had an undeniable influence on Matisse and Picasso. It has not meant that these painters slavishly reproduced African masks; rather it has meant that their horizons were broadened. It has obliged them to reinvent space, to come up with a new way of looking at things, a new language.

The themes tackled in plays, novels and films are becoming less diverse. They are characterized by the emotional experience which they reflect and the modes of expression which they use. The relative unity of the materialistic civilizations tends to restrict art to a set of related themes and contents.

Hence the African cultural renaissance derives less from the realities of an increasingly universal experience than from an ability to generate modes of expression which fulfil a culture, a system of thought or a body of works.

THE PROCESS OF RENAISSANCE AND ITS THEMES

The Black and African renaissance has been expressed in a number of ideas, theories and movements. It has its labels, its manifestos, some of which go back to the early nineteenth century, both in Africa and outside Africa. As Frantz Fanon has written, the resistance put up by traditional authorities and the wars of liberation are manifestations of this process. The pan-Negro, pan-Arab and pan-African movements are phases of it. The theories of African personality or Negritude, of *consciencism*, authenticity, *ujama* and renewal, each represent an attempt to give this process a body of ideas, a political doctrine, during the period of the accession to independence.

As with any endeavour to assert the freedoms of a people, a nation, a race or a class, the African renaissance movement crystallized around certain themes.

The lasting themes are those of the ethnic community and race as sources of culture.

Civilizational values are used to construct a humanistic

African renaissance and cultural issues

programme, a specific view of man's relations with nature and with his fellows.

I propose to outline these themes of the African renaissance, arbitrarily selecting some of their significant points or moments.

The ethnic theme

The ethnic theme is important if only because of the labels it has given birth to: the pan-Negro movement in America, *Cri Nègre* and Negritude in Europe. The African renaissance corresponds to a determination to accept race, in other words the specific culture of one's ethnic community, as well as the destiny of that culture. In this respect it distinguishes itself from the European renaissances, the Arab *Nahda*, the Germanic and Scandinavian *Kulturkreise*. Those movements did not have such a pronounced connotation of skin-colour. They renewed national cultures, seeking to rid them of their inferiority feelings by enhancing their language, their history, the political power of their representatives. In most cases, they strove to bring those cultures up to date in terms of a new experience, of new knowledge.

In this respect the Italian *aggiornamento* is equivalent to the French, Slavic or Egyptian renaissances. It is a cultural renewal. From within it re-adopts a national culture associated with the backward masses or relegated to the periphery by a foreign, élitist socio-cultural presence. As languages and cultures, Italian and French emerged within the area of Latin and replaced it towards the end of the Middle Ages. Russian and Arabic adjusted themselves to the scientific terminologies of the nineteenth century.

Similar movements of renewal occurred in ancient and pre-colonial Africa. Tutenkhamon re-established the cult of the Theban gods after his father-in-law, Ikhnaton had driven it out. Sonni Ali-Kolen restored the Songhai culture, to the detriment of the élitist supremacy of the Islamized Ulema in Timbuktu in the sixteenth century. The conflicts which wracked Africa in the nineteenth century, especially those between the traditional authorities, whether Islamic or not, and the Moslem reformers, were the results of similar renaissance movements, attesting to internecine cultural dissensions.

Pathé Diagne

The contemporary African or Negro renaissance is more than a simple *aggiornamento*. It strives to conquer political rights, to suppress apartheid and discrimination, to establish the right for Africans to build their own culture, to further their own view of the world. The modern African renaissance stems from the struggle against the racist colonial hegemony. From its inception, it was an anti-racist reaction; it implied accepting not simply ethnic and cultural destiny, but race—race as a historical burden in the conflict with outside powers.

Like the Asian and the white Arab, the Negro has accepted the fact of colour prejudice and racial contempt. In slavery he has suffered the harshest trials of all peoples.

The view of race found in the Negro renaissances is different. The rationalizations about the supposed inferiority of the Negro have had very little impact on a pioneer like E. W. Blyden,[1] who gives them no credence. In that respect, Blyden's attitude is identical to that of the masses or the traditional élites. In Franz Fanon's *Peau Noire, Masques Blancs*,[2] the racism which sharpens the oppressed consciousness of the Negro takes the form of political violence, of a system of exploitation. It is forcibly imposed from outside. The ideology which secretes the system is in the nature of racism. However, the colonized Negro-African remains indifferent to this properly speaking racist speculation attempting to come up with objective bases. Such an attitude contrasts vividly with the deeply traumatized behaviour of the black minorities that are exiled, reduced to servility or alienated by the preponderant European cultures. The Congolese peasant, the Kayi aristocrat or the Toucouleur marabout does not reflect about his colour. It does not obsess him, anymore than it affects the blue-eyed Kabyle who has been expropriated by the Algérois and the French.

1. *The People of Africa*, New York, 1871; *African Life and Customs*, London, 1908; *The Prospects of Africa*, London, 1874; *Christianity, Islam and the Negro Race*, 2nd ed., London, 1888; *The African Problem and Methods for its Solution*, Washington, D.C., 1890; *West Africa before Europe*, Washington, D.C., 1890; cf. on Blyden: H. Lynch, *Edward Wilmot Blyden, Pan Negro Patriot, 1832–1912*. London, Oxford University Press, 1967.
2. F. Fanon, *Peau Noire, Masques Blancs*, Paris, Éd. du Seuil; T. A. Quaynor, *The Politicization of Negritude*, South Illinois, 1967; Abiola Irele, 'Negritude et Africain Personalité', *Colloque sur la Négritude, Dakar, 1971*, Paris, Présence Africaine, 1972.

African renaissance and cultural issues

The traditional African, who is separated from the universe and the ideology of the colonizers owing to his rejection of them and to his restriction to a ghetto, neither analyses nor discusses his situation in the vocabulary and racist rhetoric that is forced upon him. In his eyes the domination, the aggression and the exploitation he is subjected to simply constitute the primary facts of reality. This explains the serenity of the nationalists who preceded and followed E. W. Blyden.[1] The Mahdi of Sudan, El Hadj Omar or Behanzin did not engage in racial debates with the European conqueror. Like Casely Hayford[2] and Ngalandou Diouf[3] later, they saw the African renaissance above all in political terms, and only secondarily in racial or cultural terms. For that matter, there were a number of Africans who advocated assimilation. The most notorious among them in Western Africa in the nineteenth century was perhaps Dr Boyle Horton.[4] He was a Negro. He accepted Western values as those of man in general. However he deemed the black man well-suited to assimilate them. In that respect, he heralded a certain type of renaissance discourse.

The theme of civilizational values

Cultural enhancement is the other main idea to inspire the movements and the theories of the contemporary African renaissance. The politico-religious nationalisms of the nineteenth-century reforms—Ethiopianism,[5] Mahdism,[6] Mouridism—strove to be cultural revolutions, like Kimbanguism. They endeavoured to assert a specific identity within Islam or Christianity in opposition

---

1. ibid., p. 9.
2. C. Hayford, *Ethiopia Unbound*, London, 1911, and *Gold Coast Native Customs*, London, 1906.
3. Ngalandou Diouf founded the Parti Nationaliste Sénégalais in 1906. He was the first black mayor of the four communes to be elected in Rufisque. He inspired the political movement which brought Blaise Diagne to the French parliament. He himself was elected deputy to the French National Assembly in 1934.
4. A. B. Horton, *Essays*, Editions Abioseh Nicol.
5. Ethiopianism, a political-religious movement which was born around 1915, later influenced the Churches of South Africa and Guinea. It reinvented a Negro mythology of Christianity.
6. Mahdism was a nationalist movement in the Sudan (Khartoum). The Mahdi, who claimed to be a prophet, unified the Sudanese sects and built up a political and military front which defeated the British and the Egyptians.

to the hegemonies which were screened by structures that claimed to be universal, but that were actually deeply marked by their origins.

Cultural enhancement came to mean two things. First, it meant bringing up to date the civilizations for which the African and the black were responsible. This would permit Africans to refute the charges that they were a people 'without history', 'without art', 'outcasts of history and civilization'. Secondly, it meant demonstrating the capacity of the African civilizations to generate specific cultures, and that in an age of profound change and crisis.

Another of the foremost themes was that of history. As early as the beginning of the nineteenth century, it became an important ingredient of the rhetoric of European-trained nationalists.

As we shall see further on, E. W. Blyden was impressed, indeed fascinated by the development of the historical societies of the Sudan. He was strongly attracted by the vast political structures which he uncovered in nineteenth-century Africa. The deep understanding which this Anglican clergyman displayed towards Islam, whose literature he studied extensively, stems in large part from the fact that he attributes a crucial role to it in the revival of the Mali and Songhai civilizations and that of the Hausa of Dan Foojo.[1]

The researches of Yoro Diaw[2] in the Senegal, of J. M. Sarbah,[3] Casely Hayford, Aggrey,[4] Samuel Johnson[5] and Nnamdi Azikiwe[6]

1. Dan Foojo, the founder of the Hausa Emirate, was a reformer, the author of a hundred-odd books in Hausa, Fulani and Arabic, a poet, a historian and a theologian. His *Kitab Al Farq* is famous as a theoretical apology of the Jihads of the eighteenth and nineteenth centuries.
2. Yoro Diaw was educated in the School for the sons of chiefs in Saint-Louis. An aristocrat from Waalo, his main writings have been published in *Annuaire du Sénégal*, 'Les Cahiers', BCH, 1870–c. 1929 (Rousseau).
3. J. M. Sarbah (1864–1900), a barrister from the then Gold Coast, defended the traditional landed property rights threatened by colonial legislation (as did Lamine Guèye).
4. Aggrey was the former vice-rector of Achimota College. He was a member of the Phelps Stokes Commission which the League of Nations sponsored in the 1920s. See Edwin W. Smith, *Aggrey of Africa*, London, Student Christian Movement, 1929.
5. S. Johnson, *The History of the Yorubas*, 1930.
6. N. Azikiwe, *Renascent Africa*, London, 1937.

African renaissance and cultural issues

in Nigeria, of L. Dube[1] in South Africa and Apolo Kagwa[2] in East Africa share the same point of view. They are manifestly intended to enhance the Western view of Africa by invoking a history—empires, institutions and epic figures—which rivals that of the conqueror.

As early as the nineteenth century, E. W. Blyden developed the theory that a Negro Egypt was the birthplace of civilization. Blyden's admirer, Casely Hayford, reiterated this idea in his book, *Ethiopia Unbound*. In 1937 Carter Woodson, a Black American historian and the founding editor of the journal, *History of the Blacks*, aired this idea once again. Léopold Senghor's works allude to it indirectly.[3] Chiek Anta Diop[4] has given it its most authoritative treatment. The same theme crops up in the works of J. Ki Zerbo,[5] E. Mveng,[6] the Nigerian historian O. Dike[7] and the Black American, Snowden.[8] The importance of history in shaping the way in which the African renaissance has been perceived has determined the paths followed by a number of African intellectuals.

'Every nation builds its future on its past', writes O. Dike. In an article entitled 'Histoire et Conscience' Ki Zerbo stated in 1957: 'Deprived . . . of his history [the Negro] is estranged from himself—you might say that he is alienated. That is indeed the case in every sense of the term.' In his *Unité Culturelle de l'Afrique Noire*, Cheikh Anta Diop observed for his part that: 'Only a real knowledge of the past can given one the sense of a historical continuity that is needed in consolidating a multinational State.'

1. L. Dube, a graduate of Oberlin College in the United States, was the founder of the Bantu-language newspaper *IMVO* around 1880. He also founded the Oblange Institute.
2. Apolo Kagwa, the historian of Buganda and East Africa, is the author of *Ekitabo kya Basekabaka*. See T. Hodgkin, *Nationalism in Colonial Africa*, London, Muller, 1956.
3. L. S. Senghor, *Poèmes*, Paris, Le Seuil, 1972; *Liberté*, 2 vols., Paris, Le Seuil, 1964.
4. C. A. Diop, *Nations Nègres et Culture*, Paris, Présence Africaine, 1954; *L'Unité Culturelle de l'Afrique Noire*, Paris, Présence Africaine, 1960; *Antériorité des Civilisations Noires*, Paris, Présence Africaine, 1967.
5. J. K. Zerbo, *Histoire de l'Afrique*, Paris, Hatier, 1972; *Histoire et Conscience Nègre*, Paris, Présence Africaine, 1957.
6. E. Mveng, *Les Sources Grecques de l'Histoire Négro-Africaine*, Paris, Présence Africaine, 1972; *Dossier Culturel Panafricain*, Paris, Présence Africaine, 1970.
7. See *Recherches d'Identité d'I. Wallerstein*, Paris, Présence Africaine, 1970.
8. F. M. Snowden, *Blacks in Antiquity*, Cambridge, Mass., Harvard University Press, 1970.

Pathé Diagne

Students of modern African thought have made a point of stressing this preoccupation with enhancing the past, this determination to use it as a basis for the ideologies of regaining identity and asserting an historically established capacity for actively producing history, for becoming its subject and not merely one of its objects.

Immanuel Wallerstein[1] has shown how history functions as a counter-argument to the colonial ideology. 'The ideological justification of cultural superiority has been one of the chief arguments for maintaining the colonial domination. The educational system was used to inculcate this ideology in the new élite.' Like Blyden before him, Wallerstein reminded the reader that 'written history in the colonial period was that of the colonial period itself'. History contributes to the ideological and political struggle. It gives the values of that struggle 'the legitimacy of a coherent past. It authenticates it. It builds confidence for the future'.

Another theme is that of the African civilizational values. It is less sentimental, more immediate and concrete than the historical theme. It attests to the colonized peoples' endeavour to maintain their cultural equilibrium in the face of changes which conquest and new technologies forced on it.

Its basic argument is that the African is perfectly adapted to his institutions, to the values of his laws, his legal system, his social relations and, more generally, the relations which he establishes with his fellows, with objective reality or with nature.

Even in those countries where the traditional forms of power have not survived the colonial conquest, the élite nevertheless continues to enhance its native institutions by investigating them. With his studies of the Senegambian peoples, Yoro Diaw, a contemporary of Blyden's, blazed the trail for an entire French-speaking élite. The highly important work of Amadou Hampaté Bâ,[2] Mapaté Diagne, Boubou Hama,[3] Hazoumé,[4] Fily Dabo Sissoko,[5] all follow in the wake of Diaw's studies. Serious analyses

1. I. Wallerstein, *Recherches d'Identité*, Paris, Présence Africaine, 1961.
2. A. Hampaté Bâ, *Empire Paul du Macina*, Paris and Kaidara, A. Colin, 1968.
3. B. Hama, *Enquête sur les Fondements et la Genèse de l'Unité Africaine*, Paris, Présence Africaine, 1966.
4. Hazoumé, *Le Pacte du Sang*, Paris, A. Maisonneuve.
5. Fily Dabo Sissoko, a politician, was a former deputy of Mali-Soudan.

African renaissance and cultural issues

of the African customs and societies were also written in the countries of northern, central and eastern Africa. Jomo Kenyatta's book on the Kikuyu[1] appeared several years after the remarkable work of pioneer scholars like J. M. Sarbah and Casely Hayford.

In fact it was in West Africa, in the traditionalist school of the Gold Coast, strongly influenced by Blyden, that this type of investigation, motivated by practical considerations, was pushed farthest.

John Mensah Sarbah (1864–1910), a barrister, published *Fanti Customary Laws* in 1904; this was followed by *The Fanti National Constitution*. Casely Hayford wrote *Gold Coast Native Institutions* in 1903, several years before *Ethiopia Unbound: Studies in Race Emancipation* and *The Truth About the West African Land Question*. *Akan Laws and Customs and the Akim Abuakwa Constitution* by a younger writer, J. B. Danquah, was published in 1928. Samuel Johnson, who died in 1909, left behind a work on his native Nigeria entitled *The History of the Yoruba*, which was edited for publication by O. Johnson in 1933.

These works on institutions and civilizational values are deliberately controversial. They take three different lines of argument.

The African institutions, these writers assert, are as worthy of scientific interest as those of other peoples. At times it is even suggested that they are superior. Athens and Rome, the birthplaces of the Western civilizations, are the favourite targets of these authors—along with the colonial powers, France and the United Kingdom.

Danquah writes:

The Romans, whose semi-civilized, semi-primitive customs are more familiar to the civilized world today thanks to that marvellous tool, writing, established a common law procedure which is equivalent by and large to the Akan procedure.

Speaking of the Fanti institutions, Sarbah states:

I have discovered that a complete system of laws linked both to the earth and to personal property existed among them (the Fanti), and

1. J. Kenyatta, *Facing Mount Kenya*, London, Secker & Warburg, 1938.

that from time immemorial it was handed down by tradition. It is better suited to Africa than our feudal, sophisticated, complicated modern legislation based on real estate and personal property. The natives of West Africa have a system of laws and customs which one would do better to re-direct, modify and improve rather than destroy it with ordinances.

As early as the turn of the century a similar reaction could be observed in the French territories. The Senegalese deputy, Carpot, voiced the desire of his Muslem constituents to retain a separate legal status along with their right to vote. Lamine Guèye, who belonged to a slightly younger generation than Sarbah's, gained his reputation by defending the traditional rights of the Lebou in the Cape Verde territories.

In Sarbah's opinion the native African institutions are better ones, 'more in keeping, as Chancellor Campbell suggests, with natural justice, equity and conscience than is English law'.

The indigenous economic institutions themselves were upheld in the face of changes introduced by the capitalist powers. The African intellectual would explain that the logic which underlies his economic order is perfectly rational. He did not identify himself with the rules which govern the relations between economic forces of the European type—the concept of which was used to analyse the pre-colonial African economy. It was explained that the prospects of the African societies were not those of European capitalism. The African economy, which is essentially an economy of self-owned means of production, is less fragmented and more closely connected to the other structures of social life, such as religion, ethics, politics or ontology, than is the Western economy. The European scientistic, positivistic or Marxist type of analysis tends to identify the African social organization with the Indo-European pattern of evolution. Actually, property—not unlike institutions and concepts—does not have the same function within the economy and the class system of the traditional African State that it has in the Indo-European model, which Marx and mainly his successors erroneously believed was universal.

The specific character of the inner logic of the native African economic institutions, the fact that the means of production are owned by the producers,[1] the relative scarcity of alienated labour and the tendency to collectivism have often inspired bold conclusions. Some students, for example, have maintained that the African experience has produced a model similar to those which European socialism has been reflecting since the last century. Long before Nkrumah, Sekou Touré, Senghor or Nyerere invented African 'communocracy' or the pre-Marxian 'African socialisms', Casely Hayford had tranquilly asserted the following: 'In the family system of the Fanti and the Ashanti, we have the solution to all the evils which contemporary socialism is attempting to remedy.'

Enhancing Negro art and literature was the major concern of the generations of the 1920s and 1930s, the period of the birth of such concepts as Negritude, *Cri Nègre* and the *Renascent Negro*. I will return to this theme below. But at the turn of the century it was still peripheral. Negro art had not yet gained world-wide fame. African literatures in foreign languages did not yet exist. The Bantu Xhosa-speaking writer Thomas Mafolo—the author of *Chaka*—was about the only major name known before 1930.

Education, however, which is the corner-stone of any collective renaissance enterprise, had become a central concern as early as the period being discussed here. Open to the new languages, cultures and goods being brought in from the outside, the traditional élite of the hinterland and the colonial commercial centres began to take an interest in education. It realized the capital importance of having an updated educational system based on purely African tools, languages and cultures. The constitutional measures taken by the Fanti and the Ashanti of the Gold Coast in the middle of the nineteenth century were to play a major part in the quest for an African school. It was no accident that one of the first great African experts on education, K. Aggrey, was a native of the Gold Coast. Ethiopia under Menelik II and Egypt at the time of the Nahda followed in the same path. Liberia and Sierra Leone founded institutions of higher learning as early as the 1850s. Almost from the beginning—as was to happen later

---

1. In the self-owning mode of production, the producer controls production (essentially) and the means of production. In the non-self-owning mode of production, the producer has no control over production and the means of production.

Pathé Diagne

under the colonial régimes—a conflict emerged between the advocates of cultural nationalism who were anxious to adopt the body of native traditions (men like E. W. Blyden), the partisans of straightforward assimilation into the European linguistic and cultural tradition (such as Dr Africanus Boyle Horton in Sierra Leone), and the champions of acculturation, who strove to adapt the African difference—personality, Negritude or Africanity—to the French, the British or the Portuguese identity.

The positions in this debate about the socio-cultural, educational and politico-economic example of Europe were clearly drawn by the second half of the nineteenth century. As we shall see later, this debate continues to be a central issue in the contemporary evolution of Africa.

In view of developing a purely African education, African thought itself was examined. Its moral and philosophical values, and its religious content, were carefully scrutinized. Its ability to adapt to modern science and to modern life, and its epistemological worth, were probed and compared with the processes of European thought. These concerns were always indirectly present in the works of the forerunners of the African renaissance. Despite increasing Europeanization, this area of investigation nevertheless tended to be glossed over. Frobenius outlined the geographical areas and the types of civilization. Marcel Griaule and his school, the Ruandese scholar Alexis Kagamé, and Father Tempels proceeded according to the same point of view. Negro-African thought was examined and interpreted. Attempts were made to uncover religious, philosophical, epistemological and logical systems.

The findings of these studies are frequently controversial. Despite their favourable approach, the scope of these studies remains somewhat limited owing to the biases of their authors. The influence of Islam and Christianity on them, the impact of Western philosophy distorted the presentation of their material.

The modernist African élite does not expend the same degree of effort on this field as it spends on enhancing the history and the artistic and literary works of Africa. It was not until 1968 that, organized by A. Diop, the first colloqium on traditional religions was held. The analysis of Negro-African thought as an ethical or philosophical entity, as accumulated learning, has been haphazard.

African renaissance and cultural issues

In Central Africa, where it has been pushed farthest, it has been the Church and foreign anthropologists who have done so. The latter have discovered and described, often in terms of their own particular interests, a field that is still vital and crucial to the cultural equilibrium of the masses, but that has made but a small impact on the Westernized intellectual. Despite the fact that they are extremely important, the studies of Cheikh Anta Diop, Amadou Hampaté Bâ, Boubou Hama, Alexis Kagamé, Léopold Senghor and J. Mbiti continue to be neglected. The 'existence of an African philosophy or body of thought' is still being questioned. The contemporary African intellectual endeavours mainly to demonstrate his ability to absorb modern science and knowledge, which he generally ascribes to the West and which he thinks he must equal in order to 'succeed'.

Thus, the different forms taken by the African renaissance are the consequence of hegemonic political structures implicit in colonization and institutionalized racism. Where cultural enhancement is concerned, this renaissance has tended to select and prefer some areas over others. From its beginning, race or ethnic community, history and the political freedoms have been constant themes. The more recent contribution of art and literature is connected with the appearance of the African mask in Western art and with the European infatuation with Negro music and choreography. The emergence of poets and later novelists writing in the Western languages has been the logical conclusion of a certain period of history. There is a progression in the appearance of these themes, an historical succession, each phase of which seems to bring a new dimension to the issue of cultural affirmation. The functions of the different themes and the particular order they succeed each other in are not arbitrary. They correspond to definite reactions. Racism gave rise to the racial theme. The consciousness of political oppression produced the determination to carry the struggle to the political field. The charge that was levelled against the Africans, that they were non-Promethean and a-historical, resulted in the assertion of African history, of the black man as the subject of history. The epithet 'primitive' spurred the African to excel in the most sophisticated arts of the West: poetry, the novel, 'classical' music and choreography. The terms 'irrational' and 'pre-logical' encouraged an inclination for abstract speculative reasoning. The myth of the diploma and academic distinctions inspired an academic cult all the more readily that those distinctions conferred advantages within the social system.

Confronted by European supremacy the African élite gradually came to focus its obsession on the white man and the European. Unavoidably, it reduced the world to the conflict, the dialogue between the 'white man' and the 'black man'. Until the Bandung Conference, the Asian had vanished from the élite's field of vision. Or if he was present—along with the rest of the world—it was only in the minds of the Marxists and the trade unionists, whose ideology bids them look beyond the superficial appearance of colour.

A common error among the historians of the African renaissance has been to present its movements and thinkers in a linear sequence. This approach does scant justice to a more complicated pattern of evolution. The fact that the tags and concepts which designate the different movements cover a number of diverse tendencies contributes greatly to the confusion. These reductions are sometimes rather serious.

It would be wiser to analyse the themes, the contents and the meanings of the various movements and different thinkers in such a way as to assess their contribution, the real import of their works and activities within the historical phases in which they appear. Blyden, Sarbah, Garvey, Du Bois, Césaire, Nkrumah, Senghor, Azikiwe, Leroy-Jones, C. Anta Diop, Fanon and Cabral attest to mutual influences, often simple confluences. Their arguments sometimes overlap; at other times they may be irreducibly opposed on identical issues. The same is true of the movements. They reflect various rejections and admissions. Pan-Negroism as the enhancement and theorization of the issue of race varied in importance from Blyden to Senghor, from Du Bois to Nkrumah and Sékou Touré. Pan-Africanism in the strict sense, taken as a continental prospect, shed its purely racial connotation on becoming political. The concept of African Personality evolved upon contact with the ideologies and realities of militant and multiracial Africa in the colonial period, the period of national independence and of the Organization of African Unity.

African renaissance and cultural issues

TRENDS: THE THEORIES AND MOVEMENTS

The early period

The thought of E. W. Blyden towers above the early period. Blyden sums up his age singlehandedly. He marks what can be considered the beginning of the modern Negro and African renaissance. Because of this training, because of the terms which he introduced into the discussion which he inaugurated, because of the audience he gathered, because of the breadth of his thought and its impact, because of his remarkably coherent work and, above all, because of his eminently original view of things, he clearly deserves to be called a pioneer of this renaissance. Despite its limitations, his approach is still being talked about in connection with African development and cultural revolution. Indeed Blyden originated a type of global thinking which appears as an alternative to the traditional African humanism which collapsed in the period of resistance to conquest.

Blyden was contemporary with El Hadj Omar, Samory and Shaka. Like a number of distinguished European-trained intellectuals of his period, he was of Afro-American stock. Born in St Thomas during the first quarter of the nineteenth century, he eventually settled in Liberia and Sierra Leone where he was a clergyman and professor. An inveterate traveller, he spent time in Latin America, Venezuela, the United States of America, Europe and India. He was a friend of Gladstone's, the British Prime Minister. He arrived in Africa towards 1850, at the time when El Hadj Omar and Samory were building their empires and resisting colonization. In those days Liberia and Sierra Leone constituted a zone of exchange between the representatives of the Chief of the Wassulu and the native bourgeoisie of the European centres of trade. Blyden was particularly impressed by the traditional political and intellectual élite in that area, and was at once drawn to the civilizational values which it upheld. He became familiar with the centres of Segou and Kankan, learned of the reputation of Medina and Timbuktu. Meanwhile, as we shall see later, he remained close to the common people, and was particularly interested in the thought of the village-dwellers, probing its wisdom and analysing its depth. Such broadmindedness betokens the temperament of a man of the cloth. In Blyden's case, perhaps, it is mainly due to his acquaintance with the most illustrious civilizations.

Blyden read and spoke English, Arabic, Spanish, Latin, the Liberian languages, Greek and French. He was a member of several learned societies in Europe and Asia. His fame was international.

His life-work was to develop a system of humanism that would be a reply to the challenge set by scientific progress and, more specifically, by Islam and Christianity, both of which claimed to supply a basic scheme of reference on the African continent. *Christianity, Islam and the Negro Race* is a significant book from that point of view. It reflected a widespread concern among the black Christian and Muslim peoples. In South Africa, for example, Nehemia Tile founded the Tembu National Church independently of the racist Afrikaner church. In November 1892, Magena Makone established the Ethiopian church in Pretoria. The idea of a Christian pan-Negroism was making headway. Contacts were made between the African continent and the American Negro methodist church, which had been founded as early as 1816. In 1898, M. Turner, the bishop of that church, visited South Africa to establish ties there.

Blyden's respect for Islam determined the direction that his studies took. Though he never abjured Christianity—he was in fact a Protestant minister—he felt an intense admiration for Islam, an admiration which he never bothered to hide and for which he was often upbraided. Everywhere he saw the millennial imprint of Islam on African life, which he cited as an example to the new élites. In the Christian and Islamic humanisms he saw an order of discourse which claimed universality, but was in fact ethnocentric and alien to Africa. He believed that all scientific, artistic and religious thought has to be expressed in a people's own specific terms. To his mind, Christianity and Islam were originally perceptions proper to the Indo-European white man who believes in a single deity; they nevertheless could be expressed in a purely African idiom and order of symbolism.

One has to look beyond Blyden's apparently mystical

African renaissance and cultural issues

assertions. Behind his minister's facade, he displays a 'positive', scientific and, on occasion, even 'materialistic' approach to history. He never bases his view of difference and distinctiveness on anything other than the changing forms which peoples give to their institutions according to their 'climate' and 'soul' (both Blyden's terms). Take the concept 'soul' in its historical determination, and you have a terminology that is not much different from that of Karl Marx and his contemporary positivist philosophers.

Blyden no more discourses on the equality or inequality of races and cultures than did Samory and El Hadj Omar. He assumes that the issue of man's essential unity has been settled once and for all. Instead he turns to what seems capital to him: the question of difference. One might say that consciously or unconsciously he extended the Negro-African approach which postulated cultural irreducibility within the imperial régime. To the same degree that the Indo-European state and body of thought tend to centralize and to destroy difference, the more-or-less Islamized pre-colonial African powers were apt to restrict any attempt at unification to the political sphere alone.[1] Blyden does not automatically adopt this latter view or the tradition which it expresses. None the less his approach comes remarkably close to it. He sees the Negro and African renaissance as an assertion of difference. To allow difference as the expression of distinctiveness does not mean that you must have a closed society. The author of *Christianity, Islam and the Negro Race* makes this point perfectly clear. He writes: 'It is true that culture is one and the general affects of true culture are the same.'[2] True, he adds, the Negro understanding of Islam, Christianity or progress (today one might add Buddhism and Marxism) will differ in its fine shadings from that of the European, the Arab or the Asian. Each separate understanding manifests the characteristic viewpoint and *soul* of its civilization. And yet the basic truths which are variously apprehended and put into words remain unchanged. The differences in shading simply translate the

1. The Pharaonic, Mandingo, Ashanti, Wolof and Yoruba empires embraced communities which remained autonomous. Each caste or local or cultural group retained its separate structure. Cultural conflicts were even institutionally channeled in jokes and humorous stories which have far-reaching implications on the level of human relations.
2. E. W. Blyden, *African Life and Customs*, London, 1908.

fact that truth is independent. Truth is as universal as is the capacity to neutralize it. When Blyden speaks of Christianity or Islam, he is perceiving them as historical realities which characterize certain peoples as they are seeking a deity. He believes that the black cultural experience need not include grasping the religious truth by means of the very same terms of mediation or the same representations as those adopted by the Anglo-Saxon white, the Latin Christian or the Arab Semite.[1] Blyden takes astonishing liberties with the orthodoxies of his day. He suggests that, rather than truth itself, it is the language of truth that distinguishes the various humanisms from each other. His thought is a compromise between the 'historical', physical or environmental explanation of difference (as C. Legum[2] points out) and the usual mystical explanation. The race or *soul* which transmutes truth and reality in accordance with its distinctiveness exhibits an 'essence'. There is a Negro essence, an Islamo-Arab essence, a Judeo-Christian essence. Each expresses in the language of faith a distinct form of the same divine truth. 'The whole of mankind is a vast representation of the Deity.' To illustrate and to explain difference and its vital character, Blyden continues:

Every race . . . has a soul and the soul of a race finds expression in its institutions, and to kill those institutions is to kill the soul—a terrible homicide. Each race sees from his own standpoint a different side of the Almighty. The Hebrew could not see or serve God in the land of the Egyptians. No more can the Negro under the Anglo-Saxon. . . .[3]

This statement is not made with any intent to denigrate the Egyptian Negro, the Jewish Semite or the Anglo-Saxon. Blyden believed that the individual belonging to a culture manifested his distinctiveness in the full use of his emotional, psychological and rational powers. In this way Blyden replies to the epistemological question raised by the theoreticians of so-called primitive, savage, emotive, archaic or non-Cartesian thought. His conception of

---

1. E. W. Blyden, *Christianity, Islam and the Negro Race*, 2nd ed., London, 1888.
2. C. Legum, *Panafricanism*, New York, Praeger, 1963; *Africa: A handbook to the Continent*, New York, Praeger, 1962.
3. E. W. Blyden, *West Africa Before Europe*, London, 1905.

difference excludes biological or psychological inequality. It assumes no hierarchy.

The mistake which Europeans often make in considering questions of Negro improvement and the future of Africa is in supposing that the Negro is the European in embryo—in the undeveloped stage—and that when he shall enjoy the advantages of civilization and culture, he will become like the European, in other words, that the Negro is on the same line of progress, in the same groove with the European but infinitely in the rear.[1]

The Negro will assimilate modern knowledge, which is neither white nor black, without being impaired by it, without turning into a copy of the European.

'No amount of training or culture will make the Negro a European; on the other hand, no lack of training or deficiency of culture will make the European a Negro.'[2] The African has simply developed his culture from his own standpoint. Nor could he do otherwise, for

It is true that culture is one, and the general effects of true culture are the same, but the native capacities of mankind differ, so that the road by which one man may attain to the highest efficiency is not the same one that will lead another man to success. . . .

Each race is endowed with peculiar talents and watchful at the last degree is the Creator over the individuality, the freedom and the independence of each. In the music of the universe each gives a different sound but is necessary to the grand symphony. There are several sounds not yet brought on and the feeblest of all is that hither to be produced by the Negro, but only he can furnish it. And when he does furnish it, in its fullness and perfection, it will be welcomed with delight by the world.[3]

Blyden's analysis of the Negro's distinctiveness, of his ability to renew and develop his culture and to naturalize its progress, proceeds from a compromise between mysticism and a positivistic optimism that is rather in the spirit of the Church and the age. Blyden seems much nearer to the scientism and relativism of the eighteenth century than to the historical materialism of Marx,

1. Blyden, *Christianity, Islam and the Negro Race*, op. cit.
2. ibid.
3. ibid.

Pathé Diagne

who, although he was his contemporary, seems to have put idealism and Western philosophy in its place much sooner than he. Blyden is never able to free himself entirely from the alienating allegiances of his century's thought. Nevertheless, he appears a figure of decisive break, in the sense that he chose his own ground and his own terms. Unlike some of his contemporaries and many of his followers, he viewed the issue of renaissance from a point of view that was chiefly internal.

Through his concept of distinctiveness, Blyden in his way is a pan-Negroist. He does not construct a purely racist or racial ideology. His pan-Negroism is essentially cultural; only accidentally is it 'racial'. He is not unduly preoccupied with colour and skin pigmentation. They seem to him inconsequential. The real conflict to his mind lies in the confrontation of irreducible humanisms. Blyden visualizes a united universe, but a multiethnic and multicultural one. 'The Negro race has yet its part to play, a distinct part in the history of humanity and the continent of Africa will be the principle scene of this activity.'[1] To play this part and contribute its full potential Africa must be liberated from oppressive aggression.

Changes of vast importance have taken place in the interior of Africa as a result of internal of individual intelligence and energy but instead of being perpetuated they have been destroyed by hostile influence. . . .[2]

Blyden often reiterates the theme of continentality, that is to say the theme of Africa as the hearth of the black peoples' renaissance. He also stresses the need for freedom, the necessity of releasing the inner forces of the civilizations of the continent so as to transform them. Unlike the proponents of acculturation and assimilation (like his contemporary Boyle Horton), he believes that a renaissance that is not 'soul-killing' must rest on original forces and an original heritage. Speaking of the African cultures of his period, he declares:

Without the aid or hindrance of foreigners . . . they [the African peoples] are growing up gradually and normally to take their place in the great

1. Blyden, *Christianity, Islam and the Negro Race*, op. cit.
2. ibid.

African renaissance and cultural issues

family of nations . . . a distinct but integral part of the great human body who will neither be superior Europeans, bastard Americans nor savage Africans, but men developed upon the base of their own idiosyncracies. . . .[1]

The African renaissance as it is conceived by Blyden depends on the independent growth, the putting down of roots, the rejection of assimilation, the renewal and the shaping of Africans by means of a system of education that is adapted to the native soil while serving as a vehicle for progress.

The notion of autonomy inspires Blyden to stress the necessity of accepting the institutions and values bequeathed by the past.

The African must advance by methods of his own. He must possess a power, distinct from that of the European. It has been proved that he knows how to take advantage of European culture and that he can be benefited by it. . . . We must show that we are able to go alone, to carve our own way.[2]

Blyden is resolutely opposed to the transfer to African soil of social, economic and cultural institutions which have been shaped to answer the needs of European society. What he says about Liberia in his day can be applied to the African States after a decade of independence:

We must not be satisfied that, in this nation European influence shape our society, our policy, make our laws, rule in our tribunals, impregnate our social atmosphere. We must not suppose that Anglo-Saxon methods are final, that there is nothing for us to find out, for our own guidance, and that we have nothing to teach the world.[3]

The above passage, which is contemporary with Liberia's independence, is prophetic, a formulation of the desirable process of decolonization. Its warning against the co-option of rights and freedoms by cultural imperialisms and outside linguistic,

1. ibid.
2. Legum, *Panafricanism*, op. cit., p. 20.
3. E. W. Blyden, *The African Problem and the Method of its Solution*, Washington, D.C., 1890.

Pathé Diagne

institutional or technological influences, is equally topical. Assimilation, says Blyden, poses the gravest threat to the emergence of a Negro personality within European dominated society.

It is painful, in America, to see the efforts which are made by the Negro to secure outward conformity to the appearance of the dominent race. . . . The Negro, unconsciously, imbibes the white man. . . . The only virtues, which under such circumstances he develops, are, of course, the parasitical ones.[1]

Addressing those Liberians who had turned towards the West—as do now a majority of the élites of the young African States, with their faith in 'foreign co-operation' and technical assistance and their fascination with the accomplishments of Europe—he urges them to adopt a more serene attitude, to make a greater and more creative effort:

We look too much to foreigners and are dazzled almost to blindness by their exploits, so as to fancy that they have exhausted the possibilities of humanity.[2]

Self-rule and self-confidence will only be possible, in Blyden's opinion, if the African is at peace with himself and with the reality of his existence. Without his roots he can never hope to be balanced. The African renaissance is unthinkable outside of the culture, the language, the history of the masses—outside of the institutions which the people build according to their own needs and which they control internally. Well before Cabral—who invited the foreign-educated modernist élites to commit symbolic 'suicide' so as to support the masses in giving birth to a purely African sociocultural reality—Blyden, in his inaugural address at the University of Liberia, declared:

Now if we have to make an independent nation, a strong nation, we must listen to the songs of our unsophisticated brethren as they sing of their history, as they tell of their traditions, of the wonderful and mysterious events of their tribal or national life, of the achievements of

1. Blyden, *The African Problem and the Method of its Solution*, op. cit.
2. ibid.

what we call their superstitions; we must lend a ready ear to the Kroumen, to the Pesseh and Golah men, who till our farms; we must read the compositions, rude as we may think them, of the Mandingoes and the Veys.[1]

In Blyden's day Liberian society, dominated by an oppressive, Westward-leaning Afro-American élite which was full of contempt for the indigenous urban or village population, constituted a perfect laboratory for observing certain problems which are once again found in the independent African States of today. Indeed, the Liberian Afro-American élite heralded the bureaucracy of the present, which exists independently of the masses and whose only relations with them are those of manipulation and exploitation. It was Blyden who first stressed the need for smashing the neo-colonial structure which the indigenous élite consolidated upon seizing, if not full power, at least a portion of the political machinery. He asked the Liberian élite of the nineteenth century to

study our brethren in the interior who know better than we do the laws of growth for the race; we see among them the rudiments of that which fair play and opportunity will develop into important and effective agencies for our work.

Blyden believed that the humanism of the Negro peoples could only be rooted in the African continent, in African culture, and in a modern system of African education.

Blyden took pains to point out that the renewal of knowledge consists, not in transplanting, but in naturalizing. Basically it means absorbing new frames of experience, not new expressions, idioms or languages which uproot and kill soul.

When we receive impressions from without, we must bring from our own consciousness the idea that gives them shape; we must mold them by our own individuality. Now in looking over the whole world, I see no place where this sort of culture for the Negro can be better secured than in Africa. Where he may, with less interruption from surrounding influences, find out his place and his work, develop his peculiar gift and powers.

1. Legum, *Panafricanism*, op. cit.

Pathé Diagne

Nowhere is the ground more favorable for training the Negro youth upon the basis of their own idiosyncracies with a sense of race individuality, self respect and liberty.[1]

At no time does Blyden reject the possibility of being open to outside influences. He even believes that openness is a necessity:

The African at home needs to be surrounded by influences from abroad, not that he may change his nature but that he may improve his capacity.

The Europeanization and denaturalization of the African by the British, French or Portuguese schools is, to his mind, the most destructive crime ever to be committed against the Negro peoples. He says that

the Western methods rob the African of his nationality and turn him into a slave of an alien way of thinking, an alien view of the world.

Long before the reforms in the teaching of African geography, history and literature, long before the more or less superficial Africanization of the post-colonial schools and universities, Blyden observed:

We have young men, who are experts in the geography and customs of foreign countries, who can tell all about the proceedings of foreign states in countries thousands of miles away. They can talk glibly of London, Berlin, Paris and Washington, know all about Gladstone, Bismarck, Gambetta, but who know nothing about Musahdu, Medina, Kankan or Sego only a few hundred miles from us. . . .[2]

Blyden weighed the destructive effect of memorizing European texts, parroting European ideas and values. His comments on this topic influenced Casely Hayford, who wrote:

The precise problem of education of the African is to develop his powers as an African. . . . The methods which have been generally pursued . . . have been absurd . . . because they have been carried on without the study of the man and his intellectual possibilities . . . producing, as a rule only caricatures of alien manners.

1. Legum, *Panafricanism*, op. cit., p. 264.
2. E. W. Blyden, *Presidential Address*.

Blyden repeatedly stresses the alienation of the élites who are integrated into schools and universities which teach European culture and the European languages.

Studying in Europe, the African finds himself alienated from himself, and from his countrymen. He is neither African in feeling nor in aim. He does not breathe Africa through any of the lessons he has imbibed. The smell of African ground is not in them but everything is Europe and European.[1]

The impoverishment of African and Negro humanism was the direct result of the Africans' absorption into alien cultures and outlooks, Blyden believes. One cannot abandon the language and outlook of one's culture, which make for its richness and originality, without falling, like any mere imitator, into empty commonplace truisms and clichés. His criticism of the literary output of the assimilated black American élite is still to the point. The Afro-American intelligentsia in his day was frustrated because the derivative literature it was producing met with general indifference not only among the white audience but also among the black masses. It had turned its back on the possibility of a true literary, artistic and intellectual renaissance, one closely connected with its own cultural and linguistic heritage and based on the common people.

Yet the black American writer of the period wrote in an English which he had remodelled, after five centuries, into an idiom which he really mastered. Blyden's observation is even more strikingly to the point when applied to the contemporary African *literati* writing in non-African languages. It defines perfectly the situation of the artist who has turned to an alien culture and attracts a foreign audience, in most cases solely for anecdotal or exotic reasons. The American writer before Langston Hughes and Richard Wright could be compared to his present-day African colleague. Neither his technical skill nor his mastery of a formal, academically-pure English, which he felt obliged to write in, ever gained him many admirers.

1. E. W. Blyden, *Correspondance*, Lagos, 1896. Quoted in Quaynor, op. cit.

It is the complaint of the intelligent Negro American that the white people pay no attention to his suggestions or writings; but this is only because he has nothing new to say. Let us depend on it that emotions and thought, which are natural to us, command the curiosity and the respect of others far more than the showy display of any mere acquisition, which we derived from them and which they know depend more upon memory than upon any real capacity. Let us do our own work and we shall be strong and worthy of respect; try to do the work of others and we shall be weak and contemptible . . .[1]

The pan-Negro and pan-African movements

The issue of an African renaissance, which Blyden was the first to raise, opened whole new vistas. It paved the way for a serious consideration of a modern African humanism based on the civilizational values of the continent. The author of *Christianity, Islam and the Negro Races* was very influential at the time when the liberation struggles matured. He is still topical today, now that the African states are defining policies of cultural renaissance.

A period of centralism and growth

Between the end of the nineteenth century and the period of national independence, the fact that the African peoples had no sovereignty resulted in the enterprise of African humanism being restricted to the level of theory and ideology. Up to 1920 the African and black peoples tended to assert themselves somewhat blindly in emotional outbursts and in more or less successful attempts at organization within the framework of religious, political or lay cultural associations.

W. E. B. Du Bois, who is one of the best historian of this period, described it as the moment of centralization of the racial effort and of the renascence of the racial front.

Blyden, in the nineteenth century, had had the opportunity

1. Quoted in Legum, *Panafricanism*, op. cit. Casely Hayford repeats this opinion: 'The African in America is in a worse plight than the Hebrew in Egypt. The one preserved his *language*, his manners and customs, his religion and household goods, the other has committed *national suicide*.'—In Hayford, *Ethiopia Unbound*, op. cit.

to study at first hand the problems inherent in building a Negro African State (Liberia). A highly gifted man, he was able to design a political course adapted to a technologically backward, culturally, politically and racially oppressed people. His stroke of genius was to have seen that the freedom of the Africans depended in the long run on renewing and updating a traditional system of humanism. Blyden's political failure and that of the Liberian State itself, which had very early become a sort of colonial annex administered by an assimilated élite isolated from the masses, momentarily transformed his ideas into an impossible dream.

In Liberia, the African élite which Blyden had hoped to sway continued to look to the West and remained deaf to Liberia. In the other African States the élite had either been colonized or was politically helpless. Between 1890 and 1920 the intelligentsia constituted by men like Sarbah, Hayford and N'Galandou Diouf was powerless, as were the Afro-American intelligentsias in the United States, Brazil, Central America, Cuba and the Caribbean. Within a system over which it had no control, the African élite endeavoured to emancipate itself by struggling for political rights and the mere right to exist. Along with that struggle there were, to be sure, attempts to assert a certain personality, but these did not automatically imply a programme anywhere as vast or as independent as Blyden's.

The Haitian, Liberian and Ethiopian bourgeoisies made no serious efforts in the way of a renaissance. Antonin Firmin, who wrote his essay, *De l'Égalité des Races*, in 1881 as a reply to Gobineau, and Hannibal Price, the author of *La Réhabilitation de la Race Noire par la République de Haïti*, were merely content to repeat Blyden's views. The movement which they launched in Haiti was a very limited endeavour to rehabilitate the Negro, and nothing more. In Ethiopia, Menelik II laid the foundations of a true renaissance but, owing to the structures of his Empire, nothing came of it. He fought with his neighbours to establish supremacy over that part of Africa, but he took no measures to encourage a new system of humanism. However his failure was not total, witness Ethiopia's military successes against Italy and its survival as an independent State. As for the cultural and national revolutions led by the Mahdi in Sudan and Dyn Pasha, the Tunisian

Prime Minister who founded the Collège Sadiqi, neither of them survived colonial conquest. Nor, for that matter, did any of the various politico-religious movements of the period.

Constantly ill at ease, the African élite that lived between 1860 and 1930 sought stability and self-respect in political associations. In South Africa there emerged the first Bantu nationalist organization (the Bantu Congress) under the leadership of J. L. Dube and Dr Seme, both of whom had been educated in the United States and were influenced by Booker T. Washington and W. E. B. Du Bois. The Niagara movement was born in 1912. In the French African territories, the first political organization to be founded by the native urban élite was N'Galandou Diouf's turn-of-the-century *Parti Nationaliste Sénégalais*. In the Gold Coast, J. M. Sarbah inspired nationalistic sentiments which eventually resulted in the creation of the National Congress of British West Africa in 1920. Casely Hayford was an active member of the latter organization.

As for the Afro-Americans, owing to their isolation and to the fact that they had no geo-political space of their own, they were more motivated than their African brethren to try and establish the 'racial front' which Blyden had mentioned and Du Bois had spoken of at the end of the nineteenth century. As early as 1897 and well before the Niagara Manifesto the latter had called for the foundation of a 'Pan-Negro' movement. The term is noteworthy both for its essentially racial connotation and for its lack of any geographical reference. It is an indication of the direction in which Du Bois's ideas and those of the American blacks were moving. Despite everything, the urbanized American Negro was growing accustomed to his surroundings. He was no longer necessarily thinking of going 'back to Africa'. As a front-line victim of discrimination he tended instead to forge what Du Bois called 'a coloured man's emancipation front'.

Originally Du Bois' pan-Negro movement differed from Blyden's continental pan-Negroism. The latter explicitly stated the necessity of re-creating a black political, geographical and cultural homeland. Du Bois naturally started out as an integrationist. He wanted the black to be accepted; he called for egalitarian, multi-racial institutions. But under the influence of his contemporaries, and perhaps that of Blyden himself (who died in 1912), he moved towards pan-Africanism, in the strict sense of the term. The conference which can be considered the birthplace of the pan-African ideology and movement was organized by Silvester Williams, a native of Trinidad. Du Bois was its secretary general. Later Du Bois himself organized the Pan-African Congresses. The history of these assemblies sheds light on the conflict which arose almost from the first between a more or less pan-Negro continental pan-Africanism and a more or less isolationist pan-Negroist trend.

The first tendency gave rise to Garveyism in the United States; the second produced the concept of African personality. The pan-Negro current spawned nationalist as well as integrationist or assimilationist renaissance programmes within the black diaspora. The Renascent Negro, the Niagara, New Negro, Black Power, Black Muslim and Black Panther movements are all part of this tendency. *Cri Nègre* and Negritude are its products too, or its extensions. Perhaps the pan-African idea is in the better position to rally different opinions. Taking under its wing both the isolationist or assimilationist pan-Negroism and a pan-Africanism that is less ethnic than continental, it commands considerable attention.

The pan-African movement played a crucial part in the history of the renaissance ideology on the African continent. Major ideologists and theoreticians have echoed its ideas, directly or indirectly, whatever their tendency or rallying cry. The pan-African atmosphere of Du Bois, Langston Hughes, Marcus Garvey and George Padmore pervades Towalu's *Cri Nègre* group, Casely Hayford's and Aggrey's WANC nationalists (the forerunners of Azikiwe, Kenyatta and Nkrumah), the Negritude poets (Damas, Césaire and Senghor), A. Diop's Présence Africaine movement and the various unclassifiable ideologists like Cheikh Anta Diop and Franz Fanon.

Convened in 1900 by H. Silvester Williams, the first pan-African conference was not attended by a single African delegate. Nevertheless, to it we owe the concept and the term 'pan-Africanism'. It was here too that for the first time the idea that 'the problem of the twentieth century is the problem of the colour line' was voiced from a pan-Negroist point of view. Du Bois, who adopted the pan-African idea with this meeting, also accepted its continental implication. Thus he proposed establishing in the Congo 'a great central Negro State of the world'. Later Du Bois organized the series of pan-African congresses whose history is well known. The first was held in Paris in 1919, and it was addressed by Blaise Diagne, a black deputy in the French National Assembly. For the first time it was attended by African delegates. The founders of Casely Hayford's African National Congress of British West Africa sat in on it. The slogan 'African for the Africans' made its first appearance. This latter tendency was encouraged by the emergence, between 1919 and 1920, of Garveyism, which advocated not only unity but also a return to Africa of the far-flung black people. The second congress, which was held in 1921 in London, Brussels and Paris, marked a step forward. Under the influence of the Marxists and of Du Bois, the movement embraced the principle of solidarity between struggling peoples and classes, irrespective of colour. Du Bois explicitly upheld the ideal of inter-racial co-operation, as he had done in his early days. He declared that the beginning of wisdom in inter-racial relations lay in establishing political institutions among the oppressed peoples. 'The habit of democracy must be made to encircle the world.' At the same time, the internal divisions of the movement began to appear clearly. The influence of the different nationalities on their citizens or colonized subjects increased the ideological contradictions between pan-Negroists, pan-Africanists, cultural nationalists and Marxists.

Lisbon was the site of the third Pan-African congress in 1927. Du Bois tried to hold the fourth congress on African soil, in Tunis, but failed; the congress was convened in New York in 1929. The fifth congress which took place in Manchester in 1945 was historical, its secretary general was Nkrumah. Jomo Kenyatta played an active part in it, and George Padmore, who had broken with the Comintern, was one of its principal organizers. Casting an eye on the growth of the pan-African movement, the latter declared that the most significant aspect of the fifth congress, compared with the earlier meetings, lay in its popular character. 'Representation was drawn from the ranks of political organizations to trade unions and farmers' movements.'[1] The intellectual minority which had led the movement up to then was replaced by a new leadership.

This was the congress that demanded independence in the following terms: 'We demand for Black Africa autonomy and independence.' The spirit of the Bandung conference was heralded in these words:

Before long the people of Asia and Africa would have broken their century old chains of colonialism. Then as all nations, they would stand united to consolidate and safeguard their liberties and independence from the restauration of Western imperialism as well as the dangers of communism.

This text gives one a clear idea of the conflict which had arisen in the movement, of the reluctances and approbations which divided it on the eve of the Cold War. This did not prevent a large number of intellectuals, groups and tendencies from participating in it and being marked by it. The impact of the pan-African congresses was very real. Even those thinkers who kept their distances from the movement, even those who never even participated in it directly, were nevertheless swayed by the ideas which it aired.

As yet, no really satisfactory study has been made of the pan-African movement and its different tendencies. Its internal conflicts and their ramifications and evolution are still unclear. George Padmore, Kwame Nkrumah and W. E. B. Du Bois have each given their version of the story, but they were too involved in it to be able to reveal it in full. The major historical studies of the various pan-African currents are restricted to the mere events; the views they give are fragmentary. In most cases they are reductive academic simplifications.

The political programme of renaissance

When Kwame Nkrumah and George Padmore organized the first Conference of Independent African States in 1958, both men

---

1. G. Padmore, *Pan-Africanism or Communism*, New York, Doubleday Anchor Books, 1972.

believed that the dream of pan-Africanism had, at least in part, at last become a reality. The independence of the Gold Coast, renamed Ghana, made the idea of a State policy of cultural renaissance at last feasible—and indeed urgently topical. The pan-African ideal took a new turn. It was no accident that during this meeting the concept of 'African personality' was resurrected by Nkrumah, who urged its adoption very strongly. This development, it should be remembered, occurred against a background of struggle throughout the African continent, struggle which meant playing down the concept if not the reality of ethnicity. Padmore was careful to point out on this occasion that,

Anyone is an African, regardless of race, creed or colour, if he acts right that is, if he believes in one man, one vote and in economic, political an; social equality.

A political programme of African renaissance having finally become possible with the accession of the ex-colonies to independence, the politicalization of the cultural issue took on a new dimension. The Congress of Black Writers and Artists, which was held in Rome, demonstrated that fact clearly The new turn could be seen as well in the recent thought of Sékou Touré, Nyerere and the African politicians in general, and in the writings of Frantz Fanon, Aimé Césaire, Léopold Senghor, Kwame Nkrumah and Cheikh Anta Diop The concept of an African renaissance had passed from the stage of theories and ideas to that of government practice. It had become a nationalized ideology.

A Marxist tendency existed in the pan-African movement in the United States and especially in Europe: it was represented by George Padmore, Prince Towalu, Lamine Senghor, Ramantjo, Kouyate Garang and the *Race Nègre* and *Cri Nègre* group. This current never had a name. It is still influential today among the young generations of Africans. Had it gained power somewhere it might have made a significant impact on the concept and the issue of renaissance, which now seems to rest entirely in the hands of the African heads of State.

Under the leadership of Alioune Diop, Présence Africaine undoubtedly played a part in shaping the renaissance. It provided a forum for Césaire, Fanon, Cheikh Anta Diop, Léopold Senghor, J. K. Zerbo, O. Dike, Behanzin, A. Ly, M. Diop, A. Moumouni and E. Mveng. It has been incorrectly identified with Negritude. Actually the latter is but a current, and a more or less homogenous one at that.

Invented by Aimé Césaire, the term Negritude was popularized by Léopold Senghor, who gradually came to stand for a whole body of ideas associated with it.

Kwame Nkrumah enshrined the concept of African personality, which had been used early in the century by intellectuals of the calibre of O. Awalowo, Nnamdi Azikiwe and Jomo Kenyatta. Nkrumah gave it an even wider currency than the concept of 'consciencism', which had also been advanced as a slogan for the renaissance ideology in the modern African State.

Justifiably, other thinkers and political figures formulated their own approach to the renaissance issue, such as 'Authenticity', '*ujamaa*' or 'renewal', each of which proposed its own programme of cultural development and its own vision of the self-respecting African or Negro taking his place in the modern world.

It is difficult to predict the future of these various concepts and their practical aspects, as difficult as it is to predict the future of the different nameless but by no means insignificant intellectual tendencies which have been shelved momentarily because as yet they have not gained access to political power.

The issues raised by the concepts of 'authenticity', 'renewal' and '*ujamaa*' are all present in the certainly no more expressive notions of 'African personality' and Negritude. The latter have simply been around a little longer. They have already come to stand for bodies of ideas, texts and even theoretically based government programmes which have mobilized public opinion.

According to George Shepperson[1] the concept of African personality was probably coined in 1902 by Edward Blyden, a relative of W. E. Blyden. James S. Coleman confirms this point in his book, *Nigeria: Background to Nationalism*.[2] Blyden used

---

1. G. Shepperson, 'Notes on Negro American Influences', *Journal of African History*, 1960.
2. J. S. Coleman, *Nigeria, Background to Nationalism*, Berkeley, University of California Press, 1958.

the term in a speech delivered on the occasion of the inauguration of the African Church, which had been founded by the Nigerian Majola Agbebi, who had wanted to build a strong independent African Church in the line of Ethiopianism. Blyden describes Agbebi's work as evidence of 'Africa in struggle for a separate personality'.[1] The term was born. It stuck, in much the same way that Negritude stuck after it had been coined in 1930 by Aimé Césaire in *Cahier d'un Retour au Pays Natal* and before it was erected into theory by Jean-Paul Sartre (in 1948) and redefined by Léopold Senghor in the period of national independence.

It was Nkrumah who gave 'African personality' its current prominence and political significance. At the time of the All-African Peoples Congress, it was used to rally the Ashantis, the Zulus and the Arabs within the framework of decolonization. It stepped on no one's toes. It is easy to see why Alioune Diop, like Frantz Fanon a great advocate of conciliation, adopted it as 'the foundation and basis of our humanism'.[2]

Sékou Touré too appropriated the expression. In this book, *L'Avenir de l'Afrique dans le Monde*, he wrote:

The issue is that of our Africanity, that is to say our personality. The question is one of quietly and harmoniously building an Africa that will be authentically African.

W. E. Abraham, the philosopher from Ghana, and one of the men who contributed to the elaboration of Nkrumah's 'consciencism', traced the growth of the concept of personality in *The Mind of Africa*, published in 1962. In their public statements the African politicians and statesmen have acknowledged the relevance and the importance of African cultures in the process of national reconstruction. As for African personality, that is to say the body of ideas and attitudes which are identical and equally important in all of the otherwise different African cultures, the various African heads of State seem to abide by the principle that in the future they will adopt only those attitudes and ideas which have been authenticated by the African cultures and the African experience.

1. Quoted in Quaynor, op. cit.
2. *Présence Africaine*, May, 1959.

In his speech formally opening the first session of the Organization of African Unity, Haile Selassie reminded the assembly that the world was not created all at once, that millions of years ago, civilizations flourished in Africa unsurpassed in any way by the civilizations on the other continents, and that consciousness of their past was essential in defining their personality, their identity as Africans.

Here African personality embodies what Fanon, in the same context, called 'the idea of a national consciousness', which had to be given prominence, he believed, over all other considerations.

Senghor's examination of the same concept in Addis Ababa at about the same time produced a further refinement. Senghor too stressed the importance of history. He said:

That which unites us goes back further than history, it goes back to prehistory. It has to do with geography, with ethnology, and, beyond that, with culture. Its existence is older than Christianity or Islam. It is prior to all colonizations. This community of culture is what I would call Africanity.

Senghor has repeatedly described the latter idea, contrasting it with Negritude.

The concepts of African personality (*personalité africaine*) and Africanity are gradually becoming universally accepted.

As for the concept of 'consciencism', which was invented by Nkrumah to convey his personal conception of African personality, it is not being adopted quite as widely. The same is true of Senghor's Negritude, Mobutu's 'authenticity', and the ideas of Sékou Touré, Kenneth Kaunda, Julius Nyerere and Nasser on socialism and African nationalism—owing no doubt to their political connotations and controversial implications.

Consciencism, as Martien Towa made a point of emphasizing, was the first attempt at formulating a modern African political philosophy. It is primarily a Marxist discussion of philosophy and a critique of Western thought.[1] However, 'consciencism' is not an ideology of decisive break. It does not begin with a critical

---

1. *Conséquence*, a periodical which began appearing in 1974 under the editorship of P. Hountonji reflects this point of view with some reservations.

analysis from the philosophical standpoint of the African experience properly speaking. Nkrumah's attitude is that of the European-trained African thinker. His approach does not lead to a critical rediscovery of a particular philosophical thought. Nor does it deal with the issue of 'African alienation'.

Nevertheless, in the last chapters of *Consciencism*, Nkrumah examines the recent sociological studies on the African continent, and the premises which he draws within the framework of a modern political philosophy continue to be vitally important. In the conclusions he reaches about the components and internal contradictions of African society, Nkrumah sounds a good deal like E. W. Blyden. He sees Africa as being torn between tradition, Islam and Christianity. Nevertheless Nkrumah's renaissance ideology is solidly based on scientific socialism. Of the latter he says:

Its value is universal. On the intellectual, cultural and institutional levels, it constitutes an offensive against all aspects and forms of colonialism and neo-colonialism.

Negritude as an ideology and political programme for an African renaissance was given shape on African soil by Léopold Sédar Senghor. In a series of writings, Senghor gradually elaborated a conception of the Negro and the African which constituted a coherent system of thought. It did not, however, necessarily reflect all of the ideas and orientations of the original Negritude movement as it was conceived by its various founders, who continued to claim membership in it.

The best historians of the movement are the Negritude poets themselves. Damas, Césaire and Senghor have often traced the broad outlines of its history, citing the influences and personal encounters which presided over its birth.

As I have said, the notion of Negritude was used for the first time by Césaire in *Cahier d'un Retour au Pays Natal* in 1933. In 1948, Jean-Paul Sartre outlined a theory of Negritude in his introduction to Senghor's *Anthologie de la Nouvelle Poésie Nègre et Malgache de Langue Française*. During the 1930s, Damas, Senghor and Césaire constituted a literary movement. They published a review, *L'Étudiant Noir* and inevitably they were marked by the atmosphere of the period. Thus, they were not immune to the Afro-American current of pan-Negroist and pan-African thinking; and indeed they were quick to acknowledge its positive contribution. Then too, they were influenced by the more politically-coloured ideas of their elders, Towalu, Lamine Senghor, Ramantjo, Kouaté Garang and Émile Faure, who had rallied around *Cri Nègre* and the review, *Légitime Défense* (founded and organized at the time by E. Leroy, J. Mounerot, R. Menil). The latter groups had Marxist leanings. Towalu, who was married to a black American pianist in Garvey's circle, and Lamine Senghor had founded the Ligue de Défense de la Race Nègre (LDRN) in the 1920s. They had published a journal called *Race Nègre*, which was eventually succeeded by *Cri Nègre*. Several years later, under the guidance of Lamine Senghor, along with Towalu and George Padmore, a veteran militant of the anti-colonialist stirrings of the period, the LDRN was replaced by the Comité de Défense de la Race Nègre (CDRN). Lamine Senghor addressed the anti-imperialist congress in Brussels with Sun Yat-sen and Ho Chi-Minh. Along with Kouyaté Garang, he had a considerable influence over the emigrant African workers living in France, to protect whose interests the two men founded a union. The Negritude poets also had close links with the black American writers, such as MacKay and Langston Hughes, who visited Europe at the time that the American Negroes themselves were laying the foundations for a literary renaissance. Mac Kay's *Banjo* influenced Damas, Senghor and Césaire. It incidentally gives one a good portrait of the members of LDRN and CDRN. Thanks to their organization, their publications and actions, both groups were representative of the mainstream of the black élite in France between 1920 and 1939. It was in their journal that Léopold Senghor placed the announcement of the founding of *L'Étudiant Noir* in France (1934), which, according to the announcement, aimed at establishing a cultural association in France. *L'Étudiant Noir* followed a line that differed somewhat from that of *Légitime Défense*.

The Second World War put a damper on these activities. They resumed at the end of the war, however, spurred on by a number of important events. In 1944 *Cahier d'un Retour au Pays Natal* was published in translation in Cuba. Senghor brought out his *Nouvelle*

Anthologie de Littérature. André Breton, the high-priest of sur-realism, wrote a preface to a new edition of *Cahier d'un Retour au Pays Natal*, which appeared in 1951. Sartre wrote 'Orphée-Noir' as an introduction to Senghor's 1948 *Anthology*. Here was the first critical appraisal of the work of the French-speaking black poets. Sartre's approach laid the groundwork for the ideology of Negritude.

Présence Africaine was founded in the post-war years (1947) by a group of pioneers under the leadership of Alioune Diop, who defined its objective as follows: 'It is a tool meant to serve African culture, and specifically Black African culture.' Later, the Société Africaine de Culture was born: it brought together the Negro élites of Africa and the diaspora. Most of the prominent African and non-African black intellectuals contributed to it: Frantz Fanon, Rabemananjara, Cheikh Anta Diop, Richard Wright, Fily Dabo, Aimé Césaire, M. Andrade, Amadou Hampaté Bâ, J. Ki Zerbo, A. Ly, J. Price-Mars, J. S. Alexis, P. Hazoumé, and others. Little by little, the Présence Africaine movement became clearly politicized. Many of its leaders soon came to play important roles in African politics. As early as 1945, Senghor was elected a deputy to the French National Assembly. Rabemananjara and Césaire became deputies too. Alioune Diop was appointed a member of the Conseil de l'Union Française; Price-Mars, ambassador. Présence Africaine organized the first Congress of Black Writers and Artists in Paris in 1956. The second congress was held in Rome in 1958.

The Negritude current represented by Senghor, Damas and Césaire emerged into the open as the ex-colonies gained independence. It took on a new dimension with Senghor's accession to power. A theoretician in the line of E. W. Blyden, Senghor drew up the first policy of cultural renaissance on African soil. In this connection his thinking took a new turn, as exemplified by a text which he wrote in 1956 on 'the spirit of civilization or the laws of Negro-African culture'. In it he situated his own ideas within the perspective of a renaissance which 'will be brought about less by politicians than by Negro artists and writers'.

In this text Senghor analysed the distinctiveness of Negro culture and developed his theory of difference as a legitimate basis for a black renaissance. The originality of the black man, according to the author of *Éthiopiques*, arises from precisely those features that set him apart from the European: 'Europe is the civilization of discursive reasoning, of analysis and mechanical genius.' The Negro on the other hand is characterized by 'emotion, intuition, rhythm'. The Negro is a 'rhythmic being'. He is 'rhythm incarnate'. Senghor notes that: 'It has been in the area of rhythm that the Negro's contribution has been most significant.'[1] Examining the aesthetic bases of Negro-African poetry, Senghor adds that it is rhythm which makes for its uniqueness. 'The essential quality of the Negro poetic style is rhythm.' In describing the Negro in this way, Senghor gives us his idea of Negritude. Not without reason, some critics have compared his views with those which the African ethnologists have developed in the field.[2] Others cite the influence of Sartre's existentialist formulation of Negritude. Price-Mars, however, had spoken of the epistemological distinctiveness of the black man in similar terms. Thus, in his book, *Ainsi Parla l'Oncle*, he had written:

Blacks have a sensory intelligence which is as yet ill-adapted to abstraction. . . . In them the intellectual phenomenon is altogether overshadowed by the emotional aspect.

Compare this with Senghor's remarks:

The nature of the Negro's feelings and emotivity explain the latter's attitude towards the object which he perceives with such an essential violence. It is an attitude of abandon which readily turns into an attitude of active communion, if not identification, as soon as the object's action—I was going to say personality—is strongly felt.

Senghor's Negritude bases difference and distinctiveness on a 'Negro essence'. It is an apparently timeless essence, which seems by and large unaffected by historical allegiances. This theoretical approach has been frequently criticized. Senghor's own most recent

1. Senghor, *Liberté*, Vol. 1, op. cit.
2. See *Les Critiques de d'Arboussier*, A. Ly, M. Towalu, Th. Melone, R. Menil, S. Adotevi, H. Aguessy, A. Sine, and others. See 'Bibliography'.

comments do not seem to indicate a break with these earlier opinions. Witness his reply to Faouzi.[1] The latter makes a double error, according to Senghor, in

believing in the superiority of discursive reason, which has been given paramountcy up until now by the Europeans, over intuitive reason which has been preferred but not exclusively practised by the Negroes.

For that matter, in Senghor's latest work one discerns a tendency to bring the issue up to date. Perhaps the text which gives one the clearest glimpse of this development is *Problématique de la Négritude*, Senghor's introduction to the colloquium on Negritude held in Dakar in 1971. It is a basic text which takes up the question of how to formulate a strategy for a renaissance within the framework of national independence. It expresses a reaction, a response to a discussion which had arisen during the Algiers Pan-African Festival concerning the then-current cultural problems of Africa and the whole issue of an African cultural policy.

Senghor expatiates on the theme of Negritude. In line with Aimé Césaire, he redefines Negritude as 'the simple recognition of the fact of being Black and the acceptance of this fact, of our destiny as Blacks, of our history and of our culture'. Senghor adds:

Negritude is a fact, a culture. It is the sum of the economic, political, intellectual, moral, artistic and social values, not only of the peoples of Black Africa, but also of the Black minorities in America, Asia and Oceania.

The text is not always in perfect agreement with Senghor's interpretation of Césaire's concept of Negritude. It can also be objected that, while the Afro-American continues to cultivate his original artistic heritage, it does not necessarily follow that, given his contacts with European capitalism and with slavery, he can continue to enjoy the same relationship with nature, with economic products or with man for example, as the village Ibo or the inhabitants of Poto-Poto enjoy.

The urbanized African who is caught in the texture of capi-

1. See *Jeune Afrique*, Festival d'Alger, M. Farouzi, 1969.

talist social structures already differs so radically from his brother in the interior that the immutability of the diaspora Negro as it is described by Senghor leaves one rather sceptical.

Perhaps it is easier to agree with Senghor when he says:

The task which the militants of Negritude have assigned themselves is the task of assuming the civilizational values of the Black peoples, of bringing them up to date and if need be of fertilizing them with alien influences. These values must be experienced in and for oneself, but they must be made real also in and for others. Only thus will the contribution of the new Negroes to world civilization be realized.

It is clear that, from E. W. Blyden to Cheikh Anta Diop, W. E. B. Du Bois, Nkrumah or Fanon, this general idea has been unanimously accepted. When all is said and done, the latter writers would probably only quarrel with the term that designates this idea, namely Negritude. Indeed, owing to its history, the term can be deemed too exclusive, too full of connotations and practical implications which are debatable both as to their form and their content. As a concept pan-Africanism embraces that which is designated by Negritude. The same can be said for the universal 'pan-Negroism' that Du Bois had advocated around 1897. What we have here of course is the old controversy, which is not simply due to the ambiguity of the various terms and connotations from one language to another, but which ultimately springs from different and sometimes irreconcilable assessments of the basic issue.

The most useful aspect of this issue of Negritude is perhaps the attempt undertaken by its most illustrious proponents to reconstruct the history of the literary movement of Negritude. It also provides one with a clear definition and a precise terminology of the concepts which predominate in the various pronouncements by the theoreticians and political overseers of the Black African renaissance.

Senghor rightly proposes distinguishing between 'Negritude', 'Africanity' and 'authenticity'. The viewpoint of Negritude is a universal one. Africanity, on the other hand, is equivalent to African personality or Africanness. It designates the Negro, Arab and Berber components of Africa. It stands for the sum of the African civilizational values, the body of qualities which make up the distinctiveness of the African personality. Africanity, says Senghor, means the acceptance of a fact; it also means the determination to build, by means of an African renaissance, a humanism that will be distinctly African and yet open to the rest of the world.

Authenticity is no less a felicitous concept. A. Sékou Touré and Mobutu Sese Seko use it concurrently with African personality. The President of the Republic of Guinea has observed that an African renaissance must first

take note of the fact that colonization has produced a falsification [*inauthenticité*] and a depersonalization of the colonized peoples' way of thinking. Therefore Authenticity means partly becoming reconciled with one's heritage and one's particular reality. As a step towards a renaissance, it implies destroying the colonial structures and replacing them with new structures corresponding as closely as possible to the requirements of our development and our needs.

Authenticity was popularized by the head of State of Zaire. Mobutu Sese Seko has proposed substituting what he considers a less ambiguous term, one that is less charged with partisan connotations and one that has fewer ulterior motives, for the controversial notion of Negritude. Mobutu has defined authenticity as 'the duty to think and to act independently'.

Once again we find a concurrence here, if not on the level of concepts at least on that of intentions. It is the same general concurrence one saw in Addis Ababa in 1963 when the African leaders agreed by and large (as W. Abraham points out) to stress the African's identity, to root him in his culture, to legitimize his aspirations to renewal.

Of course, it is only in practice that one can assess the adequacy of the above theories to a renaissance programme which in fact amounts to a science having its own logic and its own requirements.

This is not the place to review the various State programmes which, beyond their manifestoes, festivals, theoretical writings and colloquiums, implement the principles of an African renaissance.

'Negritude', 'consciencism', 'African personality', '*nahda*', '*ujamaa*', 'renewal', 'authenticity' and 'pan-Africanism' are all emerging to a greater and greater extent as official ideologies. Their purpose is always to liberate the African and to restore his identity and creativity.

The African renaissance is a long-range task. It is perhaps too early to reach a definitive opinion about the results thus far obtained or even about the validity of the objectives voiced thus far. After a decade of national sovereignty in Africa, the issue of African culture continues to be a vital one. In the following pages, I will try to outline a strategy for a renaissance in Africa.

FOR A SCIENTIFIC APPROACH TO THE AFRICAN RENAISSANCE

The context in which the African renaissance occurs gives us a clue about the kinds of effort that will have to be furnished. The issue of a renaissance presents itself in terms which are equivalent to those of a rational strategy.

Renascent Europe of the fifteenth century readapted a certain order of knowledge and a certain number of languages. Amid the rubble of the defunct Latin élite's thought and socio-cultural organization, she rediscovered her national and popular cultures. In the eighteenth century Germany and Russia went through a similar process. In its *aggiornamento*, Slavic culture assimilated a body of scientific thought which had developed elsewhere. Pushkin, Tolstoy and Gogol recreated a literature; Moussorgsky and Tchaikovsky re-established a national music. Along with Gorki, Mayakovsky and Lenin, the October Revolution posed the problem of a mutation that involved far more than a simple cultural development or a renaissance of the classical type such as occurred in France and England in the sixteenth century. The advent of the Soviets postulated a revolution which based culture on the masses and their creativity. Its objective was a humanism that would serve the point of view of the majority and not that of an élite class. Mao Tse-tung wanted to accomplish a renaissance of the Chinese culture that would be even more complex. He conceived it in terms of a Chinese Marxism. He implemented it, extended it deep into society and gave it permanence through a process which amounted to a revolution within the revolution (in the words of the Cuban slogan).

Pathé Diagne

Cuba and China, like Italy, the Scandinavian and the Slavic countries emerging from the Napoleonic or Germanic supremacy in the nineteenth century, had to go through an *aggiornamento* of decolonization. They had to remodel their culture, that is to say, their social and economic institutions, their literature and their arts sapped by political domination.

The French, British, Spanish or Portuguese colonial cultures do not unify. They impose their own social, historical and literary heritage, their educational or institutional machinery, their conception of man's relations with his fellows and with the objective world—and these things become a tremendous burden. They spawn an élite which is cut off from the masses, as was the élite of Blyden's nineteenth-century independent and Americanized Liberia. Only a truly popular culture, only institutions that can be assimilated by the masses and shaped according to their needs, only an art and a literature that releases native energies and creates a context of balanced cultural development, can bring modernity, science, democracy, economy, creativity and the spirit of universality back to the level of the people, the average man, the authentic African.

Another factor to consider is the wealth of Negro African art in its extraordinary diversity, as exemplified by the geometrical perspective of Bakuta, the figurative approach of Ife, the curved lines of the Akan heads, the high degree of expressionism of the Nok, Irkur or Sao art. Black Africa might well have lost its native statuettes and music had Muslem rule or 'idol-smashing' Christianity succeeded in eradicating its local differences to make way for the 'universalist' and reductive conceptions which they tried to implant in the Ashanti and Zulu confederations and in the multinational empires of Ghana, Tekruur, Mali, Kanem and Songhai.

Reflection on the issue of contemporary African culture calls for a certain amount of effort. First, one needs to cast off—scientifically, and on the purely rhetorical and conceptual level—specifically European terms. Second, one has to imagine—again on a theoretical level—a purely African renaissance and universality leading to a *praxis* and the establishment of an official programme liable to liberate art, the imagination and ethnic, not to say tribal and individual, creativity (in the line of what T. Melone has suggested).

The African renaissance is confronted with a cultural imperialism that has become increasingly complex, tentacular and aggressive. The preponderance and influence of the outside world have increased owing to the increasing number of contacts between peoples and the increasing permeability of national and natural borders. For this reason, Africa must not simply remain content with contemplating its own distinctiveness. The right to difference is an established fact. Absorption into another culture is the most sterile prospect of all. On the other hand cultural openness is necessary too. The Algiers festival had the merit of introducing a fruitful controversy about these points, a controversy which continues to be of vital relevance to Africa.

Invoking man's unity or alleged priorities of one kind or another, there will always be those to deny the legitimacy of a world based on difference and on the universalization of specific experience. To this difficulty must be added that of the contradictory or conflicting allegiances of the nationalistic African States, and of the pan-Negroists and pan-Arabists (whether Marxist or not), reacting to a historically reductive European way of thinking and socio-cultural context.

And yet historically the idea of a national culture and differential renaissance is fully justified.

There is no such thing as a universal culture or civilization in itself. Contemporary reality confronts different views of the world with each other, and different cultures backed by different kinds of political power. These views and cultures may serve the interests of nations, states, classes, ethnic groups, or sometimes even those of a whole race. It is an oversimplification to reduce all cultural problems to the sole level of class or ethnic community.

Integration, even national integration, stratifies people in such a way that minorities are nearly always subjected to a coercive power. The European States, which have traditionally favoured centralization, owing to a long history of upheavals and to long-standing diplomacy of balance of power and balance of territories, have had a devastating effect on other peoples. The world has been considerably impoverished by the disappearance of the Celts, the

Pathé Diagne

Basques, the Tamils, the Kurds, the Aztecs, to make room for the 'modern States' of the United Kingdom, France, India, Iraq and Mexico. Men in power continue to be obsessed by models. They level, destroy, and pollute the physical environment. They uproot peoples by introducing processes which are not attempts to adjust a traditional culture to technology, science or modernity, but are forms of violence and pauperization.

Humanism has of course little to do with 'soul', the myth of the 'noble savage', or the Rousseauistic view of the world. The problem of the survival of the Italian, Yoruba, Berber, Chinese, Bantu, Negro, American or Ukrainian cultures presents itself in terms of the relations between political forces, nations, ethnic groups and economic systems. It is a problem of balance of power.

A strategy of culture requires certain ends and certain means for achieving those ends. The traditional African experience has to be revitalized by being placed in contact with modern science and technology. It has to readjust its institutional and artistic content. At the same time it must retain those aspects of its cultural equilibrium which make for its uniqueness.

The primary objective, then, must be that of disseminating science and technology and adapting them to the specific conditions of the African cultural context. E. W. Blyden stressed this very point. Colonial conquest was the result of the military and scientific defeat of various societies in Africa and Asia which lagged far behind the European nations and cultures in the eighteenth century. This lag can be bridged only by the most up-to-date and sophisticated science and technology. New techniques must be developed in the field in order to build up the African economies. These techniques must be assimilated in such a way that they can be used, even militarily, to defend freedom. Thus there is a dialectic between the cultural, political, economic—and military—fields, a dialectic which is related to the world-context and to its conflicts and rivalries.

Naturally there is no question of yielding to the temptation of using modern science to further ambitions of political supremacy which run counter to the traditions of a continent practically without a history of expansion. On the other hand, the myth of an African tradition scorning the 'materialism of science and technology', a tradition whose vocation lies in contributing 'soul' to a world lacking in it—or in providing a 'spirituality' that loosens the steely joints of the citizens of the industrialized nations—is nothing but a myth. Perhaps it might have corresponded to reality in another context. This myth has blossomed in a world characterized by the balance of power. The individual—like the nation or the ethnic group—seeks his crutches in his own knowledge and in forms of power that may be ethical or aesthetic as well as economic.

The dissemination of knowledge among the masses means using African languages, adapted in terminology to modernity. These languages have to become the tools of the educational and scientific systems, of the political and economic apparatuses on the level of village, neighbourhood, city, region, nation or group of States.

An African-speaking socio-cultural context will have to replace progressively—but rapidly too—the foreign-language socio-cultural context bequeathed by colonialism. This change will make it possible for the African peoples to accede to scientific progress in the short run. It will restore their initiative and creativeness by giving them the complete control of their social, cultural and economic institutions. It will bring about democracy, instead of a minority or elitist culture or power.

The renaissance of the African plastic and audio-visual arts has benefited from the current prestige of African sculpture and the traditional African mask. These arts are being renewed in Lagos, Dakar and Brazzaville. Keita Fodeba's ballets have given new life to African choreography and music. Art critics like E. Mveng and N. Nketia have extended their interpretations of African works daringly far, and from frequently original points of view.

European experts have contributed a great deal to the preservation and study of African culture. As Alioune Diop wrote in the preface to *L'Art Nègre* which was published for the Dakar festival: 'One is moved by the vast generosity displayed by Europeans in enhancing and defining Negro-African art.'

Much has been said about renewing and preserving this art, and protecting the artist. But despite the remarkable work of E. Mveng, B. Enwonwu, Obama and Memel, no inside study of

Negro-African art in terms of the African aesthetic tradition as yet exists. The 'functional', 'religious', or 'rhythmic' Negro art has yet to be analysed from a simultaneously technical, aesthetic, sociological and historical point of view.

Fine arts schools are multiplying in Africa. Painters, sculptors, architects, ballet teachers and composers are graduating from them, creating, exhibiting and building. The academic vein of their works sometimes contrasts with the freedom and originality of the traditional artists and craftsmen. There are times when African ballet is facile. African painting is often a lifeless copy of European painting, spoiled by confusing influences. The measures that are proposed to remedy this situation are familiar enough.

William Fagg has suggested returning to tribal art within artists' studios or workshops, thus protecting the African artists and craftsmen from the kind of speculation that attaches itself to 'airport art' objects. He believes that traditional art will survive in its original spirit if it is associated with liturgy. MacEwen has successfully organized at Salisbury workshops where the ancient African techniques are being relearned.

A new direction for African art can perhaps be discerned in the work of Senegalese painter Papa Ibra Tall, and Nigerian sculptor Ben Enwonwu. Both men believe that Negro art must regain its global character. Similarly, architecture must no longer simply associate itself with sculpture or with painting, it must become sculpture or painting.

For that matter, the modern work of art must recover its collective function: it must not only contribute to humanize technology, it must integrate technology more harmoniously into the framework of daily urban, social or domestic existence.

Science and technology—both of which constitute modernity—are means. They mediate. Culture endows them with meaning by making use of them. Behind the American, Soviet, British, French and Chinese industrial realities, one discerns not only different degrees of scientific, technical or artistic practice, but also contrasting views and conceptions of that practice. In order to give expression to its 'Africanity', its 'authenticity', or its self-awareness, the African renaissance will have to assimilate modernity on its own terms. This implies, if not a revolution in the content of African culture, at least a profound transformation, a bringing up to date.

In the precolonial and precapitalist African village the art of making masks was a complex activity. It had its place in the moral, the religious and the social order. In so far as it was the art of a distinct period and a distinct ethnic group, it reflected the aesthetics and the economy of its moment and place. Likewise, the Ife heads refer to real Yoruba persons. They attest to a definite religious activity, social structure and political history, rather than to a purely aesthetic or gratuitous speculation. Yoruba and Bakuba sculpture had their place in the village economy; it was not the same place that Ben Enwonwu's sculpture has today in its economic context. Like Calder's or Picasso's art, Enwonwu's work is included in a system of galleries, exhibitions and sales. Picasso does not claim to be a 'witch-doctor' and Ben Enwonwu is not a 'Yoruba priest'. Both artists are conscious of the fact that they are agents of a social order in which art has become a market commodity. The Ife heads, the monuments of Karnak, belonged to a distinct world: the art and the artists which produced them had their place in an economy which is utterly unlike that of capitalist society.

The meaning and content of Yoruba sculpture—and of the Yoruba sculptor's activity—is nevertheless indicative. It helps us reconstruct a civilization which has not completely broken with its aesthetic and ethical traditions, which has a social order, a perception of art that is not yet entirely absorbed by mercantile capitalism.

It is undoubtedly in the field of verbal expression that African culture can best continue to assert its personality and reveal its distinctiveness. Hence the importance of the African languages and literatures. It is the mode of expression that distinguishes literatures, theatres, cinemas, choreographies and musics in the contemporary world. There can be no question of a renaissance—of the survival of a personality, a culture or a civilization—where the original sustaining language has disappeared. The French renaissance coincided with the emergence of French as a national language, the *aggiornamento* with that of Italian, the Grundtvig movement with that of Danish. The Soviet renaissance has given vigour to the languages of the USSR. The Chinese renaissance has done the same for Chinese and the idioms of its minorities. The unity of the

Black and African cultures and areas of civilization facilitates the advent of a renaissance which unifies otherwise autonomous minorities by means of African-speaking systems of education and socio-cultural contexts. In this respect education is a means of paramount importance. By establishing an authentic connection with their culture, their language, their literature, their art and their history, the young generations of Africans may become, increasingly as they adopt modern science and technology, efficient producers of a material and intellectual civilization from which they will not find themselves estranged.

It is no coincidence that the issue of language looms large in the minds of the most gifted writers of the rising generation. The South African author, Ezekiel M'Phahlele—a product of the Bantu school—and the Nigerian playwrights and founders of the Yoruba-speaking Mbari theatre, Wole Soyinka and Duro Lapido, all stress this point. These three writers are less cut off from their roots than are Ousmene Sembene and Camara Laye, both of whom have been moulded in a school that excluded all references to the African languages and cultures. M'Phahlele and Soyinka want a government that will make scientific teaching more available to the masses and that will make it feasible to adapt Bantu and Yoruba to modern knowledge. More deeply marked by the experience of assimilation than these writers, Camara Laye and Sembene are also more sensitive to cultural and linguistic frustration. It is natural that they place more stress on integrating the traditional African and Negro tools in the school of reality.

Benefiting from the creative activity—and the audience—of the masses, the African-language literatures must not be shunted into libraries, storehouses and collections. Thanks to the themes which they handle and the forms which they are written in, they are able to heal the breach between the modern African and the original way of thinking which reflects and gives expression to his personality. Chinua Achebe and Birago Diop are to be congratulated for recreating the African short-story in languages which were not their native tongues. More or less felicitously, they have managed to naturalize—the one in English, the other in French—a certain number of the Negro-African narrative's specific forms (such as its style of characterization, its technique of dramatization and plot development). Kateb Yacine has hearkened back to the Kabyle and Arab traditions. Ousmene Sembene has rediscovered Wolof discourse. Increasingly, young bilingual writers are joining forces with the purely African-speaking generation of T. Mafolo. This development is influencing the poetry of C. N'Daw and N. N'Ketia. Modern African theatre, exemplified by the Mbari group's experiments sponsored by Wole Soyinka and Duro Lapido, is also moving in the same direction. The new turn is being encouraged by the various local, national and pan-African festivals.

In an excellent article entitled 'Search for a New African Theatre', Demas N'Wako has analysed this development, which affects not only the theatre but also books, poems, films and radio stories. A partisan of both open and tradition-rooted cultural development, N'Wako writes:

As regards the aesthetic principles which in my opinion should guide the African artist in perpetuating the African identity in art, I would say from the outset that I am sceptical about typical styles. Nevertheless, I would insist on the necessity for the artist as an individual of creating within the specific cultural context of his society.

N'Wako's conception of the African school of theatre is original. It tends to agree with the ideas of B. Traoré, a lucid and keen-sighted pioneer in the field. N'Wako criticizes the assimilationist and overly-academic teaching of the African universities and schools for theatre, play, script and novel writing, acting, 'design', choreography and art history. Instead of stimulating mature reflection about African culture, based on appropriate texts and courses of instruction, these schools teach Greek theatre, symphonic music, the European novel or opera. Instead of inspiring new forms and new ideas, much African theatrical production has become an academic exercise based on *Macbeth* or *Antigone*.

The total theatre which N'Wako calls for is present in Duro Lapido's three Yoruba plays, *Oba Koso*, *Eda* and *Oba Waya*. These works include painting, sculpture, architecture, music and dancing, all of them integrated in a collective theatrical production. The new African theatre will not necessarily revive traditional ritual—which anyway has no more basis in present-day society.

However, like the other literary forms, it can use tradition to forge new languages and new schools of creative expression.

African thought still vehicles contents and institutions which are frequently more expressive of the daily life or the aspirations and commonsense of the man of the people than are the élitist abstractions aired by modern intellectuals.

The contemporary African economist, politician, ideologist or philosopher is often indifferent to a type of experience which could provide him with answers to the questions raised by his society far sooner than do the abstract speculations he indulges in.

The African civilizations in the precolonial and precapitalist period were not organized materially and socially in the same way that the Western or Eastern societies are structured. For complex historical and ecological reasons, their ideologies concerning man's relation with his fellows and with objective reality differ from those of the other continents.

There is a real basis for a 'communocratic' or 'presocialist' Africa, or an Africa that is 'autoproductive rather than capitalist',—or simply an Africa that is more 'community-oriented' than contemporary Europe.

However, despite the absence of capitalist or Indo-European-type ownership, this does not mean that no class exploitation or alienation exists in Africa. The capitalist structures which are at present emerging on African soil are destroying the foundations of the precolonial economy, which, in spite of everything, continues to be more respectful of man and of nature. The African social context and its ideology, removed as they are from capitalism proper, frequently retain the best and most generous portion of the traditional heritage. Based on this heritage, an economic revolution can re-establish the native social and economic institutions, the human use of nature and technology.

There are legal codes, constitutions, judicial, economic and administrative bodies of state which are better suited than others to the African prospect and cultural tradition. It is a mistake to project the European academic, military, civil, administrative and judicial systems on to African soil—for in doing so one perpetuates the colonial institution and a type of state that is ill-suited to the reality of African life.

The African self-owning producer was less dispossessed by his work than the rural labourer is or the modern urban unemployed worker. An alternative to the capitalist economy might be based on certain still-vital aspects of the precapitalist African mode of production. For example, trades and crafts are undoubtedly more human than industrial work, which fragments man's activity. The renewal might therefore begin in a scientific consideration of the human use of modern techniques and technologies. A functional architecture, a pictorial or sculptural art that is more fully integrated into the framework of daily life than Western art is, can recover the meaning which traditional culture had assigned to it. Complaints about a strictly chemical, uprooting medical practice are causing some people to turn increasingly to a multidimensional view of medicine, one that is more attentive to the context, the peripheral aspects and the profile of sickness—in other words to those very considerations which had determined the healer's practice in the past.

In its oral and written texts African history has, in a sense, reflected on its own foundations and its methods. This literature provides us with precious ground on which to erect the premises of that history's methodology.

African thought is a problem in itself. Thus far, the so-called modern African philosophy has consisted, not in examining the real content of the African's experience so as to grasp its tendencies and demystify its alienations, but in 'settling scores' with idealism and the typical anxieties of Western philosophy. The contradiction between idealism and materialism is a specific alienation of European thought, as is the anxiety over death or divine fate. These concepts do not necessarily express the deep concerns of the Asian or the Negro-African. The realities which they give expression to do not lie—or in any case did not lie—at the heart of every society's thought. The dominant European ideology has made these concepts the foundations of man's thought, of his philosophy. Despite the influence of the Indo-European religious and philosophical systems, the Negro-African continues to entertain a mono-substantialist view of the world. In this traditional approach, language, thought, human, animal, vegetable and mineral existence all participate in the same unbroken, replete but nevertheless active

Pathé Diagne

substance. Words, animals, thoughts and plants are active forces, efficient agents. The Yoruba, the Mandingo and the Bantu concur in saying that words, natural elements or eyes are as dangerous for the object as they are for the being. The Negro-African conception of death excludes any possibility of definitive annihilation of the being. Death is not barred from the world of the living. This view releases the African from the fear of death. For him, death is a reality which has another meaning, another content. It does not rack him to the point of becoming a philo-sophical obsession.

The grounds of African philosophy lie in the original content of its own specific way of reflecting. It will become modern, this philosophy, once it deals scientifically with its own alienations, its own limitations.

The enterprise of an African renaissance is not a quest for the past but a perpetuation of a living tradition. The theories and practices which underlie it may perhaps have a better chance of achieving their objectives if they view it in this light.

BIBLIOGRAPHY

ABANDA-N'DENGUE, J. M. *De la Négritude au Négrisme*. Yaoundé, Éditions Clé, 1970.

ABIOSEH, N. Negritude in West Africa. *New Statesman*, Vol. 10, 1960.

ACHEBE, C. *The Black Writer's Burden*. Paris, Présence Africaine, 1956.

ADOTEVI, S. *Négritude et Négrologues*. Paris, Union Générale d'Éditions, 1972. (Coll. Le monde en 10/18, 718.)

AGUESSY, H. La Négritude au Festival d'Alger. *Afrique Littéraire et Artistique*, No. 7.

ALLEN, Q. Negritude and its Relevance to the American Negro Writer. *The American Negro Writer*. California, 1962.

AMONOO, R. Négritude et Droit Africain. *Colloque sur la Négritude, Dakar, 1971*. Paris, Présence Africaine, 1972.

AZIKIWE, N. *Renascent Africa*. London, 1937.

——. *A Selection from the Speeches of N. Azikiwe*. London, Cambridge University Press, 1961.

BALANDIER, G. *La Littérature Noire de Langue Française*. Paris, Présence Africaine, 1950.

BEIER, U. In Search of an African Personality. *The Twentieth Century*. 1959.

BELINGA, E. Négritude et Science. *Colloque sur la Négritude, Dakar, 1971*. Paris, Présence Africaine, 1972.

BLYDEN, E. W. *Christianity, Islam and the Negro Race*. London, W. B. Whittingham & Co., 1888.

African renaissance and cultural issues

BLYDEN, E. W. *The African Problem and other Discourses, Delivered in America in 1870.* London, W. B. Whittingham, 1890.

——. *West Africa before Europe.* London, C. M. Phillips, 1905.

CÉSAIRE, A. *Discours sur le Colonialisme.* Paris, Présence Africaine, 1963.

——. L'Homme de Culture et ses Responsabilités. *Présence Africaine* (Paris), No. 24–25, 1959.

——. Culture et Colonisation, *Présence Africaine* (Paris), No. 8, 1956.

COLEMAN, J. *Nigeria: Background to Nationalism,* Berkeley, University of California Press, 1958.

COUNTEE, C. *Color.* New York, 1925.

DAMAS, L. *Poètes d'Expression Française.* Paris, Le Seuil, 1947.

DAVIDSON, B. *The African Genius.* Boston, Mass., Altantic Monthly Press, 1970.

——. *The African Awakening.* London, Cape, 1957.

DECRAENE, P. *Panafricanisme.* Paris, Presses Universitaires de France, 1971.

DIAGNE, P. *La Négritude au Festival d'Alger.* Dakar, SACSEN, 1969.

DIENG, A. A. Diogomaye—Négritude. *L'Étudiant Sénégalais,* 1965.

DIOP, C. A. *Nations Nègres et Culture.* Paris, Présence Africaine, 1957.

——. *Afrique Précoloniale.* Paris, Présence Africaine, 1960.

——. *Unité Culturelle de l'Afrique Noire.* Paris, Présence Africaine, 1960.

DU BOIS, W. E. B. *The Souls of Black Folk.* Chicago, Ill., A. McClurg & Co., 1903.

——. *Panafrican History.* London, 1947.

——. *Color and Democracy: Colonies and Peace.* New York, N.Y., Harcourt, Bruce & Co., 1945.

EWANDE, D. La Francophonie ou la Négritude Récupérée. *Afric-Asia,* 1971.

FANON, F. *Peau Noire, Masques Blancs.* Paris, Éditions du Seuil, 1952.

FROBENIUS, L. *Voice of Africa.* London, Hutchinson, 1913.

GARVEY, A. J. (ed.). *Philosophy and Opinions of Marcus Garvey.* New York, N.Y., The Universal Publishing House, 1923.

GUIBERT, A. *Léopold Sédar Senghor.* Paris, Présence Africaine, 1962.

HAYFORD, C. *Ethiopia Unbound.* London, C. M. Phillips, 1911.

HYMANS, J. *Léopold Sédar Senghor.* Edinburgh, Edinburgh University Press.

IRELE, Abiola. Négritude et Africain Personalité. *Colloque sur la Négritude, Dakar, 1971.* Paris, Présence Africaine, 1972.

JAHN, J. *A History of Neo-African Literature.* London, Faber, 1968.

JULY, R. W. *Origins of Modern African Thought.* New York, Praeger, 1968.

KESTELOOT, L. *Les Écrivains Noirs de Langue Française.* Brussel, Institut de Sociologie, 1963.

LY, A. Sur le Nationalisme dans l'Ouest Africain. *Publications. PRA,* 1959.

MBUMUA, E. *Un Certain Humanisme.* Yaoundé, Éditions Clé, 1972.

MENIL, R. Une Doctrine Réactionnaire: La Négritude. *Action.* August 1963.

MELONE, Thomas. *Négritude.* Paris, Présence Africaine, 1960.

M'PHAHLELE, E. *The African Image.* London, Faber & Faber, 1962.

NIANG, S. Négritude et Mathématique. *Colloque sur la Négritude, Dakar, 1971.* Paris, Présence Africaine, 1972.

NKRUMAH, K. *Consciencism.* London, Panaf, 1966.

SANE, A. *De la Négritude.* 1970. (Manuscript.)

SARTRE, J.-P. Orphée Noir. *Anthologie de la Nouvelle Poésie Nègre et Malgache.* Paris, Presses Universitaires de France, 1948.

SENGHOR, L. S. *Anthologie de la Nouvelle Poésie Nègre et Malgache de Langue Française*. Paris, Presses Universitaires de France, 1948.

——. *Poèmes*. Paris, Le Seuil, 1964.

——. *Liberté*. Paris, Le Seuil, 1964. (2 vols.)

——. *Les Fondements de l'Africanité ou Négritude et Arabité*. Paris, Présence Africaine, 1967.

SERPOS, T. *Négritude et Mathématique*. Paris, Présence Africaine, 1972.

SHEPHERSON, G. Notes on Negro American Influences on the Emergence of African Nationalism. *Journal of African History*, Vol. 1, 1960.

SMITH, E. W. *Aggrey of Africa*. London, Student Christian Movement, 1929.

SNOWDEN, F. M. *Blacks in Antiquity*. Cambridge, Mass., Harvard University Press, 1970.

TALL, P. I. Négritude et Arts Plastiques Contemporains. *Colloque sur la Négritude. Dakar, 1971*; Paris, Présence Africaine, 1972.

TOURÉ, S. *Guinée An I*.

TOWA, M. *Négritude et Servitude*. Yaoundé, Éditions Clé, 1973.

TRAORE, B. *Théâtre Négro-africain*. Paris, Présence Africaine, 1958.

WAGNER, J. *Poètes Nègres des États-Unis*. Paris, Istra, 1963.

WALLERSTEIN, I. Panafricanism as Protest. *The Review of Politics*, Vol. II. Chapel Hill, N.C., University of Notre Dame Press, 1960.

WAUTHIER, C. *L'Afrique des Africains*. Paris, Le Seuil, 1964.

WOODSON, C. G. *Negro Makers of History*. Washington D.C., Associated Publishers, 1958.

k